FRANCIS BACON

FRANCIS BACON

BRITISH ARTISTS

ANDREW BRIGHTON

TATE PUBLISHING

First published 2001 by order of the Tate Trustees
by Tate Publishing, a division of Tate Enterprises Ltd,
Millbank, London SW1P 4RG
www.tate.org.uk/publishing

Reprinted 2005, 2008
First published in hardback 2013

A catalogue record for this book is available from the British Library
ISBN 978 1 84976 041 6

Distributed in the United States and Canada by ABRAMS, New York
Library of Congress Control Number applied for

Designed by Webb & Webb

Colour reproduction by DL Imaging Ltd, London

Printed in Hong Kong by Great Wall Printing Company Ltd

Front cover: Francis Bacon, *Portrait of Isabel Rawsthorne* 1966
(detail of fig.33)
Frontispiece: Barry Joule, *Portrait of Francis Bacon* 1982, Bacon
photographed in 1982 standing next to a photograph of himself taken
by Helmar Lerski in Berlin in 1928

Measurements of artworks are given in centimetres, height
before width.

CONTENTS

1 INTRODUCTION 6

2 PRETEXTS FOR DESPAIR 9

3 IDEOLOGIES OF DESPAIR 21

4 BACON'S DIFFERENCE 35

5 CRUCIFIXIONS 63

6 ILLUSTRATION AND THE 75
DYER TRIPTYCHS

7 ERIC HALL AND THE POETS 83

8 BACON'S DELAY 89

NOTES 92

SELECT BIBLIOGRAPHY 94

CREDITS 94

ACKNOWLEDGEMENTS 94

INDEX 95

INTRODUCTION

AN ATHEIST, FRANCIS BACON died of a heart attack, nursed by two nuns of the Servants of Mary, on 28 April 1992 in Madrid. He was eighty-two years old. Five days before his death he had flown from London, against his doctor's advice, to visit a young Spanish friend.

Before he became famous, wealthy and celebrated in the major institutions of modern art, Bacon's style of life was established. He traversed conventions of dress and social milieux; he mixed with toffs, toughs and the intelligentsia. He used make-up. He darkened his hair with shoe polish. Sometimes he dressed in Savile Row suits (suggesting membership of the British establishment); at other times he wore a leather jacket, then the garb of bikers and hard men. Whatever his outer clothes, he was given to wearing women's tights underneath.

After his death his body was cremated and his ashes flown back to England where they were scattered in a private ceremony without benefit of Church or State. He had always refused the honours the British establishment seeks to bestow upon its renowned subjects. According to one story, he was sounded out to see if he would accept one of the highest awards in the gift of the Queen, the Order of Merit. He turned it down with great camp dignity, 'No ducky, give it to someone else, it will give them so much more pleasure.'

* * *

There have been developments in Bacon scholarship since the first edition of this book. Martin Harrison, Martin Hammer and others have explored Bacon's pictorial and particularly photographic sources. His Reece Mews studio has been reconstructed at the Hugh Lane Gallery in Dublin and Margarita Cappock and her colleagues have created an archaeology of the site where he worked for the last thirty years of his life. Other art historians have located Bacon's work more firmly within the concerns and activities of artists working in his time and in the history of Queer Culture. Bacon's own account and biographical readings of his work have been at least implicitly challenged. Further, new paintings and works on paper have emerged into public knowledge and there is the legal minefield of contested work proposed for inclusion in Bacon's oeuvre. The selected bibliography in Matthew Gale and Chris Stephens' catalogue for Tate's 2008 Bacon exhibition lists fourteen books and catalogues published since 2000. Add scholarly articles, popular books and journalism and you have an ocean of words. I have used this new scholarship when it offers considerations that thicken this short account of Bacon.

The painter Adrian Ryan used to tell a story of a night in Soho with Bacon, when entering The French pub Bacon turned to him and said, 'there's David Sylvester, what lies shall we tell him tonight?' Sylvester's interviews with Bacon continue nevertheless to be the primary text mined by scholars. However, part of the fascination and importance of *Interviews with Francis Bacon 1962–1979* is the way the artist resists the critic's insights when they get too like a stable interpretation. Bacon believed in the truth of fiction. While he has profound things to say about painting, his quoted autobiographical statements require scepticism: in the course of sociable nights buoyed on alcohol he did not let truth get in the way of a good anecdote, as the differing reported versions of incidents in his life attest. Even when sober, Bacon misled Sylvester and others about his working procedures and suppressed information about his sources. He denied he drew. He kept certain works hidden from public view. Statements by Bacon are sites for excavation rather than sources of firm evidence.

* * *

'It is not a trivial question, Socrates said: what we are talking about is how one should live'.[1] On the evidence of what Francis Bacon said in interviews you can propose his answer to Socrates' ethical question. It is that one should live with eyes wide open to the brutal facts of how we are. And how we are is without meaning. For him, if our lives are to have dignity then one must forge meaning. We must create ourselves in some compelling way. This not an exceptional view; it is a common sense of modernism.

I once stood in an exhibition of Bacon's work with its curator, David Sylvester. I asked him where is the best place to hang his paintings? Without hesitation he replied, 'in an English country house'. I take this to mean that Bacon was a transgressive artist and at the heart of what he transgressed was the house of his father. 'People forget', said Sylvester, 'Francis was a toff'. Recognition of what his work does can be developed by thinking about the pictorial, social and political house mores that he transgressed. My account of these transgressions turns on the question, how did a man brought up in the Protestant ascendancy and without art school training become one of the great pictorial cultivators of *Les Fleurs du mal*?

This account seeks to inform how one might experience, think about and value Bacon's work. However, it also provides information that could serve to devalue Bacon, by saying, for example, that he was a self-dramatising narcissist, a user of people, a political reactionary who contrived melodramatic paintings out of sordid images and *jejune* pictorial clichés. Such charges are not without purchase, but he did transmute these base materials. His paintings continue to convince as paintings; they hold their peculiar charismatic ground in the major museums of modern art. With a discerning promiscuity he soaked up past art and modern imagery. Like no one else he made the sensational vivacity of paint collide with the mechanical image. Bacon's work uses a moment in the technical development of image making and tension it set up for pictorial sensibility. This enforced the apparent violence of his work but he was a painter looking for pictorial violence.

An artist's ideas, values, milieu, their pictorial and technical resources can tell us something of how a work of art came to be made. They can serve in asking why these works were vivid and why they are still vivid. However, to recognise and cultivate pleasure in Bacon's transgressive work should not be without unease. It does pose the question, in what is one being complicit? To what is one giving value? Ought it be a part of how one should live?

1 PRETEXTS FOR DESPAIR
A CONTEXT OF DESPAIR

I was seventeen. I remember it very, very clearly. I remember looking at a dog-shit on the pavement and suddenly I realized, there it is – this is what life is like. Strangely enough it tormented me for months, till I came to, as it were, accept that here you are, existing for a second, brushed off like flies on a wall … I think of life as meaningless; but we give meaning during our own existence. We create certain attitudes which give it meaning while we exist, though they in themselves are meaningless, really.[1]
Francis Bacon, Interview 5, 1975

WHEN BACON EMERGED into major public recognition at the end of the Second World War despair was in fashion among intellectuals. Continental Existentialism conjoined with an English Neo-Romanticism that had been bemoaning the modern world since the 1930s. Friedrich Nietzsche was in vogue as a source for Existentialism. Bacon read him seriously. When Bacon says we create attitudes that give life meaning, he echoes Nietzsche's argument that after the death of God man must create himself. His dog-shit revelation is the daily epiphany of depressives. It sets the necessity of finding some drive, some source of conviction so compelling that it will motivate action despite a sense of the self and existence as being without value or meaning.

For many critics despair and pessimism were valued attributes of an artist's work. In the shadow of the atomic bombs dropped on Hiroshima and Nagasaki, the writer Osbert Sitwell could write of the work of the painter Graham Sutherland, 'a citizen of the sunset age, an Englishman, who saw the world's great darkness gathering'. At that time Sutherland was one of Bacon's closest friends, a pictorial mentor, advocate and supporter.

The most widely read British literary magazine of the 1940s was *Horizon: A Review of Literature and Art*. It had a distinguished history of covering the visual arts. In the final edition published in December 1949 there is an article by the critic Robert Melville on Bacon and seven black and white reproductions of his paintings. He attributes to them a 'glimpse of the fires of despair and frenzy'. The article sits between an essay on the Marquis de Sade by Maurice Blanchot and a short story by James Lord, 'The Boy Who Wrote "No"', a tale that ends with its subject paralysed and only able to twitch his defiance. The magazine's editor, Cyril Connolly, in his introductory comment to the edition attributes to the Marquis 'the loudest and most interminable "No" in literature – No to God, No to Nature, No to Man'. He goes on to say that 'this study in misunderstood genius leads us easily on to Bacon's horror-fretted canvases'.

The substance of Connolly's editorial ends with a paragraph in which he speaks of the modern movement's struggle in a disenchanted world, 'between man, betrayed by science, bereft of religion, deserted by the pleasant imaginings of humanism against the blind fate of which he is now so expertly conscious'. He ends with a much quoted declaration that 'it is closing time in the gardens of the West and from now on an artist will be judged only by the resonance of his solitude or the quality of his despair'.

Bacon's early paintings have been seen as reflecting the war itself and in particular the images of concentration camps that emerged as the Allies liberated Europe in the latter part of 1944. One of the reproductions in

1

Three Studies for Figures at the Base of a Crucifixion
c.1944
Oil on three boards
Each 94 x 73.7
Tate. Presented by
Eric Hall 1953

Horizon was of the triptych, *Three Studies for Figures at the Base of a Crucifixion* (fig.1). It was completed in 1944, before the publication of the photographs of the camps, and Bacon had worked on it over a number of years. Thanks to co-exhibitor Graham Sutherland, it was first shown at the Lefevre Gallery in London in April 1945 a month before the end of hostilities. While he had exhibited and been reviewed in the 1930s, this exhibition marked the beginning of Bacon gaining a substantial public reputation as an artist. His work attracted notice; its affective power was acknowledged, even if its status as art was questioned. 'I have no doubt of Mr Bacon's uncommon gifts,' wrote Raymond Mortimer in a review of the exhibition in the *New Statesman*, 'but these pictures expressing his sense of the atrocious world into which we have survived seem to me symbols of outrage rather than works of art. If Peace redresses him, he may delight as he now dismays.'[2]

But the paintings of these three malformed figures, like pacing lewd freaks caged in a bloody orange enclosure, did not simply have their origins in the horrors of war. Nor do the art-historical debts to, for instance, Picasso's biomorphic monsters of the late 1920s (see fig.14) and the horrific *Mocking of Christ* c.1510–15 (Alte Pinakothek) by Mathis Grünewald tell the whole story. That the three figures are, as Bacon declared, the Eumenides (the Greek Furies) from Aeschylus's *Oresteia* also adds connotative resonance. These were the resources for Bacon's visual articulation of an ideology, one that the war had not brought and peace would not redress. The culture of pessimism helped to nurture Bacon's recognition, but it was the context not the pretext of his rhetoric of despair. It was not the source of his necessity, conviction and motivation: their origins came earlier.

ORIGINS OF DESPAIR

David Sylvester: *Perhaps you'd tell me what you feel your painting is concerned with besides appearance.*
Francis Bacon: *It's concerned with my kind of psyche, it's concerned with my kind of – I'm putting it in a very pleasant way – exhilarated despair.*[3]
Interview 3, 1971–3

Born in Dublin in October 1909 to English parents, Francis Bacon was British but at the time the country of his birth was in the violent process of achieving statehood independent of Britain. His family were part of the Protestant ascendancy. He told David Sylvester, 'Protestants were so violent, they didn't want to think of Catholicism as being the only thing that Ireland existed by. And that's the reason that Protestants are so rabid – I was brought up as a rabid Protestant with no beliefs of course'.[4] Bacon's boozing, bullying, opinionated and gambling father 'Eddy' had made a career as an army officer. Grandson of a general, son of a captain in the Hussars, Captain Anthony Edward Mortimer Bacon had served in Ireland and South Africa, and then returned to Ireland to own, breed and train racehorses after his financially astute marriage and retirement from the army. As Anglo-Irish landlords and post-holders, Bacon's family and relatives were under threat of attack during his childhood. If Bacon had followed the conventional path of his background he might, for instance, have become a colonial official like his elder brother, with a life eased by servants and a private income over and above salary. He could have ended his days in the last bastions of the colonial way of life in southern Africa where his sisters and, after his father's death in 1940, his mother were to spend their later lives.

It was the industrially derived wealth of his mother Winifred's family, the Firths, that supported the Bacons in Ireland. Bacon referred to his father as a failed horse-trainer. The style of life of the landed English gentleman

2
Sir Alfred Munnings
My Wife, My Horse & Myself
1932–3
Oil on canvas
101.6 x 127
The Sir Alfred Munnings
Art Museum, Castle
House, Dedham, Essex

was 'primarily concerned with social and sporting activity … dominated by the horse, the single most potent symbol for the traditional aristocratic fighting class'.[5] Famously philistine and hostile to modern high culture, they did support a subculture of equestrian art. When the racehorse painter Sir Alfred Munnings attacked modern art in his presidential speech at the Royal Academy of Arts annual dinner in 1948, it was to the common sense of his clients that he appealed in his denigration. In his paintings he depicted well bred horses and people mixed in with jockeys, gypsies and others who worked around or followed the horses (fig.2). This equestrian way of life cut across the socially high and low as Bacon was able to do in his own social and sexual life. What is absent from the social world Munnings painted and his conception of art are the professional middle classes and in particular the values of the intelligentsia. To the social stratum into which Bacon was born, Munnings's work represented the acceptable face of art: an art for English country houses.

CHILDHOOD HORRORS

Bacon was the author of his own childhood. That is to say, he chose to make public stories of his childhood as a mixture of neglect, threat, violence and rejection. Published in 1964, the first book on Bacon included a brief anodyne biographical sketch. It took the form of a catalogue raisonné, a scholarly listing of his work up to 1963 introduced by the then Director of the Tate Gallery, Sir John Rothenstein, and written by the Keeper of the Modern Collection, Ronald Alley.[6] It is the kind of publication usually reserved for the distinguished near dead or dead artist. The authors and the form of the book are an indication of the influence of the gallery where he had been exhibiting his work since 1958, Marlborough Fine Art Ltd.

The publication of major biographical revelations begins with John Russell's excellent Bacon monograph in 1971.[7] Homosexual acts ceased to be illegal between consenting adult males in England in 1968 and so stories of such incidents could no longer be used as potential evidence for a prosecution. By describing his life in the way he did, Bacon contrived or at least allowed a situation to develop in which his work would in part be understood in the light of his own autobiographical stories. They became the pretext for his persona as an artist.

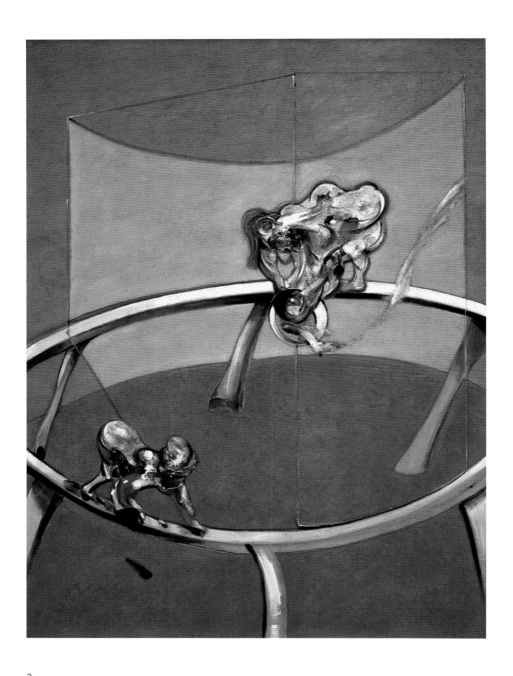

3

After Muybridge – Study   Bowl of Water/Paralytic   Oil on canvas
of Human Figure in Motion   Child Walking on all Fours   198.5 x 147.5
– Woman Emptying a   1965   Stedelijk Museum, Amsterdam

4

Eadweard Muybridge

Infantile Paralysis Child

Walking on Hands and Feet

Photograph reproduced in

Muybridge, **Complete Human**

and Animal Locomotion,

vol.II, Dover, plate 539

From his accounts of his childhood Bacon was an abused child. He claimed to have had little or no parental affection and some brutality. His parents came to detest each other. Entrusted to a local Protestant clergyman of no great academic enthusiasm, his education was desultory. Because of asthma, from which he suffered all his life, Bacon could not join in his father's equestrian activities; proximity to horses and dogs sparked acute attacks. Yet he claimed his father forced him to ride. Bacon said that he disliked his father but that he also desired him sexually. He alleged to a friend that his father had him regularly thrashed by the grooms. Only in his middle teens did Bacon attend boarding school for five terms between 1924 and the spring of 1926.

Bacon's stories are an iconographic resource for his own paintings. A kinship of deformities suggests a mother and child in *After Muybridge – Study of the Human Figure in Motion – Woman Emptying a Bowl of Water/Paralytic Child Walking on all Fours* 1965 (fig.3). The figures gambol on a racecourse fence; the down-struts bend away from the track to avoid injury to falling horses and jockeys. Further, the curved orange plane that forms the back of the irrational perspective frame is an abstracted version of the curved back walls in other paintings derived, Bacon suggested, from the shape of the windows of his grandmother's house.

THE FALL FROM FAMILY

Bacon's account of his family upbringing ends in 1926 at the age of sixteen. His father discovered him dressed in his mother's underwear and expelled him from home. Since his early teens Bacon had been an active homosexual in relationships with his father's grooms. With an allowance of three pounds a week from his mother, which was considerably more than the average income of the time and enough to live on, he departed for London.

These stories have been not only an iconographic source for him, they have also been important to the validation of Bacon's paintings. Framed within the idea that art should express the artist's 'inner most being', his known masochistic sexuality and abused childhood serve to authenticate the character of his paintings. However, Bacon's stories call for some scepticism. Michael Peppiatt, who has written the most reliable biography of Bacon, quotes from a school contemporary of Bacon who describes him as socially assured and sophisticated, interested in the turf and academically undistinguished rather than incompetent. The cruelty Bacon describes when placed in the context of his class is not that exceptional: most male members were sent away to school even before reaching their teens and many were beaten, bullied and some sexually abused.

We know that Bacon read Sigmund Freud, who may have been a source for his understanding of his sexuality and for his accounts of his childhood. Freud's essay 'The Economic Problem of Masochism' was available in English translation from 1924. In that essay Freud suggests that masochism may arise from the retention and confusion of two phases in the development of a child: parents as objects of libidinal desire and their subsequent role as lawgivers. In his discussion of what he calls moral masochism he argues that the child translates a sense of guilt into a wish for parental punishment, a wish expressed in fantasies of beatings by the father and of having 'a passive (feminine) sexual relation to him'.[8]

SEX AND ART IN BERLIN AND PARIS

David Sylvester wrote in a biographical note for the 1998 exhibition *Francis Bacon: The Human Body*:

In 1926 he left home, initially travelling with a friend of his father's with whom he spent several months in Berlin. He went on to Paris, where he started making drawings and watercolours after seeing an exhibition of Picasso drawings in the summer of 1927. In order to get some mastery of French he spent three months with a family near Chantilly.[9]

This survival of the Grand Tour when the aristocracy rounded off their offspring's upbringing sounds like an enviable piece of post-school education arranged and supported by his parents.

Bacon's stories of these years are more lurid. We know Bacon left school in April 1926 when he was sixteen, thanks to Peppiatt's research. Expelled from home, he was in London for a time but was in Berlin by spring 1927. He would have been seventeen. For both his art and his sexuality, biographers have argued, the two or three months Bacon spent in Berlin were to be significant. In the late 1920s and early 1930s Berlin was a destination for homosexual excursion: in W.H. Auden's words, 'Berlin was the buggers' daydream'.[10] A literature and a mythology grew up around the city that may have coloured Bacon's reminiscences. In Bacon's account the friend of his father was a manly man intended to show him the heterosexual straight and narrow. However, Bacon claimed, 'he used to fuck absolutely anything', including Bacon himself.[11] His deviant chaperone took him to nightclubs catering for all sexual proclivities. What is clear is that in the late 1920s Bacon lived briefly in a city that accepted his sexuality. London was not to do so until the last quarter of the twentieth century. Even in the 1930s Bacon did not hide his sexuality. Recalling that time, Patrick White remembered Bacon's 'beautiful pansy-shaped face, sometimes with too much lipstick on it'.[12] Berlin may well have been a source for the courage to 'out' himself.

Like Picasso, much of Bacon's art is about sex. For him art aspires to the condition of the orgasmic. This was not a new idea. In British aestheticism from Walter Pater to the Bloomsbury Group momentary aesthetic ravishment was prized and described in terms redolent of orgasmic pleasure. Aristotle in *De Anima* said, 'all the affections of soul involve a body-passion, gentleness, fear, pity, courage, joy, loving, and hating; in all these there is a concurrent affection of the body'. A strand in modernism is a pagan assault on the Christian idea of depriving the body so that the soul might flourish. Bacon's work purports to address body passions, not the disinterested pleasure of the aestheticist eye. In his descriptions of the responses he sought for his paintings, he frequently uses 'violent' and other metaphors of assault. Bacon seeks to 'come immediately onto the nervous system', thereby to 'unlock the valves of feeling and therefore return the onlooker to life more violently'.[13] His rather mechanical metaphors, 'nervous system' and 'valves of feeling', probably have their origin in Freud's picture of instinctual life as a mechanism of circulating energies. Nevertheless, Bacon's picture is more convulsive and physiological rather than a machinery of secretions such as Marcel Duchamp gives us in *The Bride Stripped Bare by Her Bachelors, Even*. It is to his form of sexuality that his art aspires. Did Bacon see and comprehend the work of Otto Dix, George Grosz and Max Beckmann and the photomontage of Hannah Höch and other Berlin Dadaists while he was in Berlin? A positive answer attributes to the seventeen-year-old Bacon an improbable level of cultural luck and competence. The fractured space of Dadaist photomontage, the evocation of misanthropic disgust by Grosz and Dix and the sheer pictorial ambition of Beckmann probably did help to form Bacon's pictorial vocabulary and values. However, there is little sign of such influences in his work of the 1930s, and it seems unlikely that he had any serious encounter with these artists or their work in Berlin. However, he could have seen the work of some of these artists in *Twentieth Century German Art*, a major and well publicised exhibition organised in London by Herbert Read in 1938 of artists condemned as degenerate by the Nazis.

Bacon saw an exhibition of Picasso drawings at Paul Rosenberg's Gallery in Paris in the summer of 1927. Biographers believe, partly due to Bacon's own claims, that this exhibition included some of Picasso's globular figures, which he began in 1927. They are arguably the major single art source for Bacon's work. Peppiatt, however, has pointed out that the Rosenberg exhibition did not include any biomorphic or indeed Cubist pieces.[14] It consisted of Picasso's neoclassical images. It was Picasso at his stylistically and socially most reactionary that provoked Bacon to make watercolours and drawings himself.

Bacon's stories of his traumatic childhood and early sex life may have been told for their own sake – honest and cathartic revelations and fibs – but they give us one of Bacon's pretexts. By word of mouth and in published sources his account of himself increasingly accompanied him and his work. The stories lent authenticity to his art and its rhetoric of despair. They tell us something both of how he wanted others to understand his history and of how he understood it himself. These understandings became sources for his paintings; they are in a sense part of the 'literature' on which his work drew.

5

Three Studies for Figures at the Base of a Crucifixion c.1944 (detail of fig.1) Oil on three boards Each 94 x 73.7 Tate. Presented by Eric Hall 1953

F. Bacon 29,

6
Watercolour
1929
Watercolour and
bodycolour
21 x 14
Private collection

7 (opposite)
The Studio, August 1930
Pages 140–41
Tate Archive

2 IDEOLOGIES OF DESPAIR
BACK IN LONDON

*I admire T S Eliot's poetry tremendously, you remember that essay where
he quotes Shakespeare: 'As flies to wanton boys are we to the gods –
they kill us for their sport'. Eliot says this is marvellous poetry, but bad
philosophy. But then he was a Catholic, and of course, being a Catholic
he would consider that bad philosophy. I don't think it's bad philosophy.
I think it's the way life is.*[1]
Francis Bacon, Interview transcript, 1975

BACON RETURNED TO LONDON in late 1928 or early
1929. He lived and worked in a converted garage in South Kensington. He
had furniture and carpets made to his own designs and exhibited them in his
studio. Consequently, in *The Studio* for August 1930, a brief article appeared
on Bacon as a designer (fig.7). So within eighteen months of arriving in
London, not yet twenty-one and without formal art training, Bacon had the
skill to design, the capital to have made and the audacity to have exhibited
and publicised his work as a modernist designer.

The first known painting of Bacon's, *Watercolour* 1929 (fig.6), is so
eclectic that every commentator nominates different influences: Giorgio
de Chirico, Paul Nash, the Purist aesthetic geometry of Fernand Léger
and Le Corbusier paintings (the latter's design work was a source for
Bacon's furniture), and of course Picasso. What sort of skills does this
untrained artist exhibit in the work? In terms of manual dexterity this is
not a difficult work to make: the colour is flat and much of the drawing
is ruled with a straight edge. There are no gradations of colour or tone
and no volume in space to draw. Two things are impressive: the complex
asymmetry of the composition and the grasp of both positive and negative
space. Most neophytes when they draw objects are unaware that they are

also drawing the shape of the space in which the object exists. Probably by intelligent copying, Bacon acquired a sophisticated pictorial understanding. Corroboration of this suggestion comes from John Russell's observation that one of his carpets of about 1929 was almost a straight paraphrase of a complicated Synthetic Cubist painting by Picasso.

THE ARTIST

Formative of Bacon's practice was the idea of 'The Artist' current when he became a painter. The artist as a special being with an intuitive route to their authentic personality was a cliché of the educated. In 1933 in his pioneering book *Art Now*, which included a reproduction of a Bacon painting, Herbert Read surveyed the philosophical and theoretical origins of modern art and discussed the variety of its practice, ending with the question: 'Does that leave us with any one element common to all great pictorial art, the peculiar possession of all genuine artists?' He answers this himself:

> It is the capacity to allow the personality to express itself in the craftsmanship: some mysterious equivalence between thought and action. The act of putting pencil to paper, brush to canvas, becomes an act of what Croce has called lyrical intuition, and in that act, in that instant, the personality, and indeed, the spirituality of the artist is revealed.[2]

Benedetto Croce was the most influential aesthetician of the first half of the twentieth century. He has now virtually disappeared from academic attention. An implicit function of Read's book was to establish grounds for denying the status of artist to traditionalist practitioners. He was waging war on the likes of Munnings, the Royal Academy and the tastes of the plutocracy for the cause of modern art and progressive intellectuals. Croce supplied a definition of the 'genuine' artist: someone who produces work by particular cognitive processes. The argument invites artists to present themselves as having mysterious mental characteristics, abilities that are beyond rational account and to claim, for instance, the loss of self-awareness that is typical of many acts of doing or making as 'lyrical intuition'. When in 1945 the state support for modernist art was established in the UK, the architect of the Arts Council of Great Britain, the economist Maynard Keynes, broadcast to the nation: 'The artist walks where the breath of the spirit blows him. He cannot be told his direction; he does not know it himself.'[3] The inviolability of lyrical intuition was a cornerstone of cultural policy.

The relationship between words and art is manifold. Bacon was inclined to deny that artists' words matter. He was, however, a great manipulator of his own reception. He thought and spoke about what he was doing a great deal, although, once formulated, his views apparently remained fixed; he reiterates, for instance, in later interviews ideas and phrases we first encounter in the Sylvester conversations.

He could 'cleaver the heart of a book faster than any Oxford Don', claimed his friend Barry Joule.[4] Artists of Bacon's generation were rarely systematic readers. Such a basic academic exercise as critically analysing or summarising a text was not part of their post-school education. They were not required to master texts with which they disagreed. They read literature and particularly philosophy to find sympathetic ideas and supportive and enabling arguments and exemplars. Less formally educated than many of his contemporaries but more intellectually able than most, Bacon had a selectively absorbent mind. When John Russell declares of Bacon, 'he has never finished a bad book, he has never entertained a dull thought and has never made a commonplace remark', minus the hyperbole he is describing a particularly intelligent form of this self-centredness.[5] Bacon's theorised ideology was a construction derived from wide if unsystematic reading and hearing the opinions of others better formally educated than him, filtered through an acute sense of his self-interest as an artist.

Until Bacon's death, due to his own insistence and influence, retrospective exhibitions and publications downplayed him as a painter before 1944, that is, before *Three Studies for Figures at the Base of a Crucifixion* (fig.1). He had destroyed much of his early work. What remain are the few paintings he sold or gave away during the 1930s. As if intuition and 'the breath of the spirit' created him, Bacon covered up the sources from which he acquired his cultural and art knowledge. He denied the importance of the staff, as it were, of his informal art school. There are two important figures, Roy de Maistre (1894–1968) and Eric Hall (1891–1959), older men who had the culture he needed. In the course of this book I shall refer first to de Maistre and then at the end to Hall. They tell us something of the milieu in which Bacon moved and what cultural material it offered him to work with.

ROY DE MAISTRE

When they met in 1930 Roy de Maistre was thirty-five, Bacon was twenty. An Australian, de Maistre was among the first artists in Sydney to be aware of Post-Impressionism. After the First World War he had exhibited and sold work, and taught in Australian art schools. He initially came to Europe in the mid-1920s and returned permanently at the end of the decade. He had his first London one-person exhibition in July 1930 and then showed with Bacon in Bacon's studio at the end of the year. De Maistre knew much of what Bacon needed to know. He was not only a mentor; he also became in awe of Bacon. Betty MacMurray who attended an art school started by de Maistre in the late 1930s recalled, 'Roy looked on him as one whose judgement he prized most of all. If Francis said he liked a picture, that was the final word'.[6]

Until Bacon's death de Maistre's importance to his development was underestimated. This can be attributed to Bacon. To reveal how much and what he had learnt from a mediocre painter from the colonies was less than conducive to the myth of his untaught genius whose only living master was Picasso. De Maistre was 'a homosexual of extreme discretion' according to David Marr, the biographer of another of de Maistre's protégés, the Nobel Prize-winning novelist Patrick White.[7] De Maistre became a Roman Catholic in 1949 and was to paint church commissions.

De Maistre was surprised that Bacon, who had a sophisticated appreciation of Picasso, would ask him technical questions that most schoolchildren could answer. In particular, de Maistre helped Bacon with oil painting. De Maistre was rather pedestrian in the way he painted in oils; he essentially filled in his linear drawing. The paint lacks independent life. Technically both men at that time were best in watercolour and pastels, essentially coloured drawings. Bacon's most accomplished works of the 1930s, for example *Composition (Figure)* 1933 (fig.8), combine this technique with Picasso-like biomorphic figures.

However, de Maistre's importance to Bacon's work was more than simply technical. In a painting that belonged to White, *Studio Interior* c.1931 (fig.9), de Maistre prefigures Bacon's paintings of coupling male figures observed, as in, for instance, the left-hand panel of *Triptych Inspired by*

8
Composition (Figure)
1933
Gouache pastel and
pen and ink on paper
53.5 x 40
Juan Abello Collection

T.S. Eliot's Poem 'Sweeney Agonistes' 1967 (fig.10). There were other de Maistre paintings in this genre, of 'fellas doing things to fellas', to quote his biographer Heather Johnson, which, she reports, were destroyed by the executors of his will.[8]

De Maistre's *Figure by a Bath* c.1937 (fig.11) suggests something of broader significance. The globular figure in the painting resembles Bacon's destroyed *Abstraction* c.1936 (fig.12), *Figure Getting out of a Car* c.1943 (fig.29), and the central figure of *Three Studies for Figures at the Base of a Crucifixion* 1944 (fig.1). They are the prototypes of the Furies and Harpies, the vengeful agents of guilt that reappear in Bacon's work in different forms over the years. A shared iconography is an indication of a period of such intellectual and professional intimacy that Bacon's debt to de Maistre clearly went beyond the technical.

John Rothenstein wrote of Roy de Maistre: 'Not many who know him now suspect that in the most significant sense, aristocrat though he is, he is a self-made man. His establishment in Europe, his personality as an artist, are the consequences of acts of faith and will; so too is his membership of the Catholic Church.'[9] De Maistre's claims to have aristocratic forebears and to be related

9

Roy de Maistre

Studio Interior

c.1931

Oil on canvas

50.5 x 60.6

Art Gallery of New South Wales, Australia. Gift of Patrick White 1974

10
Triptych – Inspired
by T.S. Eliot's Poem
'Sweeney Agonistes'
1967
Oil on three canvases
Each 198 x 147.5
Hirshhorn Museum
and Sculpture Garden,
Smithsonian Institute. Gift
of the Joseph H. Hirshhorn
Foundation, 1972

to the royal family were bogus. De Maistre was the son of an Anglican third generation Australian racehorse breeder whose name was not de Maistre.

JOSEPH DE MAISTRE

Roy de Maistre was baptised as LeRoi Leviston de Mestre; he changed his name to de Maistre and added Joseph to the list of his forenames in 1930, the year that he met Bacon. He claimed Joseph de Maistre as an ancestor. Patrick White, who met and became a lover of Roy de Maistre in 1936, provides further evidence of the importance of Joseph de Maistre to Roy, and to Roy's considerable influence on his acolytes.[10] In 1938 White visited Savoy with the idea of writing a novel about Joseph de Maistre. White, who was better educated and older than Bacon when he met Roy, nevertheless described Roy as formative of his intellectual life.

Count Joseph de Maistre (1753–1821) was an anti-rationalist. His theological political arguments were formed in bitter and radical opposition to the French Revolution and the Enlightenment. Whereas Enlightenment thinkers looked to reason as the means by which humanity might at least improve its condition, Joseph de Maistre considered that humankind since the Fall had lost its knowledge of the divine order: our fallen condition is inherently irrational. Isaiah Berlin wrote of Joseph de Maistre:

> Maistre conceived of life as a savage battle at all levels, between plants and animals no less than individuals and nations, a battle from which no gain was expected, but which originated in some primal, mysterious, sanguinary, self-immolatory craving implanted by God. This instinct was far more powerful than the feeble efforts of rational men who tried to achieve peace and happiness (which was, in any case, not the deepest desire of the human heart – only of its caricature, the liberal intellect) by planning the life of society without reckoning with the violent forces which sooner or later would inevitably cause their puny structures to collapse like so many houses of cards.[11]

Why did Roy choose to turn a phonetic resemblance into a claim for Joseph as an ancestor and why is this of use to an understanding of Bacon? Roy had in 1925 stayed in France with the ardent Catholic intellectual and author, William Gibson, 2nd Baron Ashbourne whose studies of the

11
Roy de Maistre
Figure by a Bath
c.1937
Oil on board
64 x 54
Private collection

12
Abstraction
c.1936
Oil on board
Probably 94 x 74
Destroyed

Abbé de Lamennais cite Joseph de Maistre as a precursor.[12] In the 1920s and 1930s Joseph was in the intellectual air. The French monarchist Charles Maurras and his counter-revolutionary political movement Action Française claimed him as an intellectual source. More significantly, he was admired by T.S. Eliot. For any non-Catholic outside France knowledge of Joseph de Maistre gave access to a Catholic vision that was fundamental to modern French literature and in particular to Charles Baudelaire.

'De Maistre and Edgar Poe have taught me to reason,' wrote Baudelaire in *My Heart Laid Bare*, which forms part of the *Intimate Journals*. T.S. Eliot gave centrality to the de Maistrian aspect of Baudelaire in his introduction to Christopher Isherwood's translation of *Intimate Journals* published in 1930:

> Baudelaire perceived that what really matters is Sin and Redemption ... the recognition of Sin is a New Life, the possibility of damnation is so immense a relief in a world of electoral reform, plebiscites, sex reform and dress reform, that damnation itself is an immediate form of salvation – salvation from the ennui of modern life, because it gives some significance to living.[13]

In a unedited version of Sylvester's interviews with Bacon, Francis says:

> I think that most people who have religious beliefs who have the fear of God are much more interesting than people who just live a kind of epicurean and drifting life ... I can't help admiring them but despising them ... if you can find a person totally without belief, but totally dedicated to futility, then you find the more exciting person. [14]

Bacon's atheism was a negative mirror of theism. He did not just not believe in God. For him the absence of God left only futility. For Joseph de Maistre humankind's estrangement from God rendered reason and hope in the rationality of human institutions futile. De Maistre was a source and an indicator of the ideological tradition that informs Bacon's work.

THE EXECUTIONER

God for Joseph de Maistre was 'an angry power, and this power can be appeased only by sacrifice';[15] 'man being thus guilty through *his sensuous principle*, through his flesh, through *his life*, the curse fell on his blood, for blood was the principle of life, or rather blood was life'.[16] An image of human sacrifice is a repeated motif in both Bacon's and Roy de Maistre's paintings: the image of crucifixion. Joseph de Maistre saw the executioner as the officiating priest at the altar of atonement. He describes the executioner's work in his most celebrated and quoted passage:

> He arrives at some public place packed with a dense and throbbing crowd. A poisoner, a parricide, or a blasphemer is thrown to him; he seizes him, he stretches him on the ground, he ties him onto a horizontal cross, he raises it up: then a dreadful silence falls, and nothing can be heard except the crack of the bones breaking under the crossbar and the howls of the victim. He unfastens him; he carries him to the wheel: the shattered limbs interweave with the spokes; the head falls; the hair stands on end, and the mouth open like a furnace, gives out spasmodically only a few blood-spattered words calling for death to come.[17]

In Bacon's paintings crucifixions figure by name from 1933 until 1965. Of the fourteen extant works before 1944, Bacon named three crucifixions. In another five paintings figures hold out their arms in a possibly cruciform way, but they appear animated and are probably derived from Picasso's *The Three Dancers* 1925 (fig.13), which, however, has been interpreted as a Dionysian scene of crucifixion.

In April 1933 a crucifixion by Bacon was included in an exhibition at the Mayor Gallery in London. Later in the same year it was reproduced in Herbert Read's book *Art Now* (fig.14); pointedly Read placed it opposite Picasso's *Baigneuse* 1929. *Crucifixion* 1933 (fig.15) depicts two figures, the first attached to a cross, the second standing on the same level attending to the other. Similarly, in *Painting* 1946 (fig.37), we look up at the foreground figure sitting before the crucified carcass; the perspective of the picture raises them up as if on a podium. If he were to stand, he would be on the same level as his victim. As in later crucifixions, the body is opened up into a bloody carcass. Someone or thing has worked cruelly upon these constrained bodies.

Bacon was a kind of realist; he sought to show the 'brutality of fact', the reality of things rather than just appearances.[18] His vision of reality denied the progressive hopes of many of his generation of intellectuals as well as the comfort of conservatism or even the possibility of redemption that was

13

Pablo Picasso

The Three Dancers

1925

Oil on canvas

215.3 x 142.2

Tate. Purchased with a special Grant-in-Aid and the Florence Fox Bequest with assistance from the Friends of the Tate Gallery and the Contemporary Art Society 1965

100. PABLO PICASSO
Baigneuse. 1929
By permission of the Galerie Simon, Paris

101. FRANCIS BACON (b. 1910)
Crucifixion. 1933
By permission of the Mayor Gallery

allowed in Joseph de Maistre's Christianity. So militant an atheist was he that when a book by a friend, the late Bruce Bernard, was on the verge of publication he stopped it because of his writing about religion and Bacon.[19] Few British intellectuals held such an overt, persistent and aggressively disenchanted view of the world. There is little precedent for it in British art and literature. Bacon starts to articulate this ideology in his early work when he was close to Roy de Maistre. Bacon's route to his sanguine images of bodies torn and constrained may have included Joseph de Maistre's terrible description of an execution.

14
Herbert Read
Art Now, 1933
Plates 100–1, showing
Pablo Picasso, **Bather**
1929 and Francis Bacon,
Crucifixion 1933

15
Crucifixion
1933
Oil on canvas
60.5 x 47
Murderme, London

16

Sam Hunter
Some very varied clippings in Francis Bacon's studio photographed by Sam Hunter in the summer of 1950. They include from left to right: (top row) photographs of Himmler and Goebbels from *Picture Post*; the aftermath of a riot in 1916, one of the injured; Velázquez's portrait of Pope Innocent X; the famous photograph of Baudelaire by Nadar; (centre row) a plate entitled 'Vaudeville Films – "Facials" and Close Ups' from *The History of the British Film 1896–1906* (London 1948) by Rachel Low and Roger Manvell; Grünewald's *Christ carrying the Cross* in the Kunsthalle, Karlsruhe; people rushing for shelter during street fighting in Petrograd, 17 July 1917; (bottom row) Rodin's *The Thinker*; a photograph of hippopotamuses from Marius Maxwell's *Stalking Big Game with a Camera in Equatorial Africa* (London 1924)
Photograph Courtesy Sam Hunter

3 BACON'S DIFFERENCE
INTO THE FIELD OF CONTESTING VALUES

Art is a method of opening up areas of feeling rather than merely an
illustration of an object ... Real imagination is technical imagination. It is
in the ways you think up to bring an event to life again.[1]
Francis Bacon in an interview in *Time*, New York, 1952

WHILE HISTORIES OF MODERN ART and the hanging
policy of museums tend to suggest a view of art as following settled lines
of development, the art world is in practice a field of contesting values and
evaluations. In discussing Bacon's work of the late 1940s to 1960s, I want
to locate it in relation to some of the then current conflicts of art practice
and criticism.

The art historian, painter and one-time Professor at the Slade School of Art,
Lawrence Gowing, commented that the impact on some painters of Bacon's
first one-person exhibition at the Hanover Gallery in 1949 was 'indescribable':

> It was an outrage. A disloyalty to the existential principle, a mimic
> capitulation to tradition, a profane pietism, like inverted intellectual
> snobbery, a surrender also to tonal painting, which earnestly progressive
> painters have never forgiven. It was everything unpardonable. The
> paradoxical appearance at once of pastiche and of iconoclasm was
> indeed one of Bacon's most original strokes.[2]

One reason for Bacon's offence was the promiscuity of his sources in general
and his use of photography in particular.

Bacon's pictorial sources traversed mediums and traditions. From medical textbooks on diseases of the mouth and positions in radiography to Michelangelo drawings, from film stills to Edgar Degas pastels and paintings, from newspaper shots of shouting politicians to Auguste Rodin sculpture, from boxing, physique magazines and Eadweard Muybridge photographs of bodies in movement to Rembrandt and Diego Velázquez paintings, from Pablo Picasso's work of the later 1920s and early 1930s to photographs he commissioned of lovers and friends, these and many other images fed his work.

The photograph of the man with a monkey shown in fig.16 was a source for *Head IV (Man with Monkey)* 1949 (fig.17), one of a series of six entitled *Head I* to *Head VI*. The dealer who exhibited the *Head* paintings in 1949 was Erica Brausen, who had just opened the Hanover Gallery. She supported and promoted Bacon from the late 1940s until 1960. She encouraged him to produce paintings for exhibitions, she worked to sell them to public and private collections, lent him money and bought his work as gallery stock. Bacon's production was spasmodic. He destroyed what he took to be failed paintings. Between the photograph of the man holding a monkey and *Head IV* may lie many destroyed canvases.

Part of the intensity of his paintings up to the mid-1950s is that they hover on the edge of obvious incompetence. Much of *Head IV* is thinly and cursorily painted. The forms of the man, the monkey and the curtain were probably drawn first in pastel onto the unprimed raw canvas, then redrawn with black paint. With a thin white line he indicates a perspective space frame at odds with the symmetry of the composition and the confines of the painting's edge. In the black wash that forms the darkness between the curtains and the back of the man the drawing is still discernible. The next conventional move would have been to build up the rounded shapes of the head and shoulders and he does begin to suggest the shoulders and back. But Bacon uses the transparency of the head and also the way the darkness between the curtains creates a hairline on the side of the head. He teases the head into three dimensions by painting an ear in highlights and indicating the side of the forehead with a small burst of white. Reasserting one of the lines of the drapery locates the front of the face. He revisits the back of the head with a scumbled white line but leaves the ghost of its previous black delineation. When he does paint the man's shoulders and back in lighter tones, he picks up the line of the right curtain by leaving a crevice of black.

17
Head IV (Man with Monkey)
1949
Oil on canvas
81 x 66
Private collection

The intelligence and courage of *Head IV* and the paintings of the late 1940s to the mid-1950s lie in Bacon's use of his own ineptitude and his limited painterly virtuosity. He exploits the seductive plasticity of silver-grey to black, giving that sense of form made by laying lighter tones onto dark. He recognises the affective power of his pictorial transgressions in his stumbling construction of conventional form and space. He grasps them and teases them into greater vivacity. This is intelligent because of his acute attention to what he is doing. It is courageous because the whole enterprise hangs on a knife-edge and is entirely reliant on his ability to find something in the paintings that saved them from looking like the work of an under-trained painter working from photographs. That, of course, is what he was. The paintings he destroyed were no doubt the paintings he thought gave him away.

18
Victor Pasmore
Spiral Motif in Green, Violet, Blue and Gold: The Coast of the Inland Sea
1950
Oil on canvas
81.3 x 100.3
Tate. Purcahsed 1953

PAINTING INTO DARK, 1949

Bacon was to develop as primarily a tonal painter up to the mid-1950s. Structuring by tone and limiting hue simplifies technical problems but it is the vocabulary of form illuminated by directional light in pictorial depth. It is the antithesis to appearance rendered chiefly by hue as in Claude Monet or Camille Pissarro. Since the Impressionists most artists have painted onto smooth, white-primed canvas. This maximises the vivacity of hue but can deprive dark tones of depth. Bacon painted onto brown unprimed canvas, onto a mid-toned ground. Before Impressionism most painters worked on canvases primed in a mid-tone. It provides a key tone against which dark and light tones are disposed. Bacon painted, in other words, as if Impressionism had never happened. In the early 1950s he started his practice of painting on the 'wrong' side of the canvas, that is, the side where the tooth of the material provides a rough texture, making the passage of the brush more explicit.

Gowing, in his account of artists' reactions to Bacon's 1949 exhibition, does not give names. However, Victor Pasmore was the pictorial and ideological antithesis to Bacon. Gowing was partly of Pasmore's milieu. Pasmore was born in 1908, the year before Bacon. He had exhibited with Bacon in 1936 when he was still making the observation-based figurative paintings he was to abandon in the late 1940s for abstraction. His first exhibition of entirely abstract paintings in 1951 made him a leading practitioner and advocate of non-figurative painting in England. Pasmore was a kind of secular Ruskinian. For John Ruskin God's order was manifested in nature, and art must aspire to express that order. For Pasmore, rather than depict nature in tone, line and hue, artists should follow nature 'in the manner of its operation'.[3] He derived his *Spiral Motif* 1950 (fig.18) from mathematical studies of nature and growth.

Pasmore tended to describe his work as guided by the logic of historical development. He abandoned figurative painting because 'the only field which appeared open to rational development was in terms of abstract form'.[4] Pasmore saw art as progressive, as evolving like and with science. Bacon's discussion of modern art was couched in terms not of art's evolution but of what it is possible to do as a painter now: history as a condition rather than a process. Pasmore seems to hold that reason and nature are in ultimate harmony. In Bacon's work human consciousness and desire are alienated from the natural world. There are conflicting natures and they are not benign.

Looking at the series of heads Bacon exhibited in 1949, Pasmore must have seen Bacon as the voice of pictorial and ideological reaction. Before a dark curtain in black, greys and blue-brown – almost monochrome – *Head I* (fig.19), *II* and *V* show mouths wide open and ape-like, with long canine

19 (overleaf left)

Head I

1947–8

Oil and tempera on board

100.3 x 74.9

The Metropolitan Museum
of Art. Bequest of Richard
S. Zeisler 2007

20 (overleaf right)

Head VI

1949

Oil on canvas

93.2 x 76.5

Arts Council Collection,
Southbank Centre, London

teeth exposed as if emitting some terrible animal cry. In *Head VI* (fig.20) the screaming mouth, teeth no longer ape-like, is a dark orifice above the purple-clad shoulders of the first of Bacon's pope paintings. It was derived from a reproduction of Diego Velázquez's *Pope Innocent X* 1650. The source for the open mouth is attributed to the mouths of two women, both at the moment before a child's death: the nurse shot on the Odessa steps in Sergei Eisenstein's *Battleship Potemkin* and the mother protesting at the murder of her infant in Nicolas Poussin's *The Massacre of the Innocents* 1630–1.

The renegade Surrealist Georges Bataille referred to the mouth as the means by which human animals express moments of extreme emotional and physical feeling. The art historian Dawn Ades has discussed Bacon, photographs of slaughterhouses published in *Documents* and the writings of Bataille, who edited the magazine between 1929 and 1930. Bacon possessed copies of *Documents*. Bataille wrote: 'On great occasions human life is concentrated bestially in the mouth, anger makes one clench one's teeth, terror and atrocious suffering make the mouth the organ of tearing cries.'[5]

The artists' reaction to the 1949 exhibition reported by Gowing was not universal. Wyndham Lewis, 'that lonely old volcano of the Right' as W.H. Auden called him, was then eking out his income by writing art reviews for *The Listener*. Arguably, his work as a painter, novelist and theorist constitutes the most important and serious confrontation with modernity by any British artist in the first half of the century. Bacon's work in the second half of the century constitutes a similar achievement. Lewis wrote:

> Of the younger artists none actually paints as beautifully as Francis Bacon. I have seen painting of his that reminds me of Velásquez and like that master he is fond of blacks. Liquid whitish accents are delicately dropped upon the sable ground, like blobs of mucus – or else there is the cold white glitter of an eyeball, or of an eye distended with despairing insult behind a shouting mouth, distended also to hurl insults. Otherwise it is a baleful regard from the mask of a decaying clubman or business executive – so decayed that usually part of the head is rotting away into space. But black is his pictorial element. These faces come out of the blackness to glare or to shout.[6]

Lewis, who rarely wrote without attacking someone, had described Bacon's paintings in an earlier article, at the same time as taking a swipe

21
Portrait of Lucian Freud
1951
Oil on canvas
198 x 137
The Whitworth Art
Gallery, Manchester

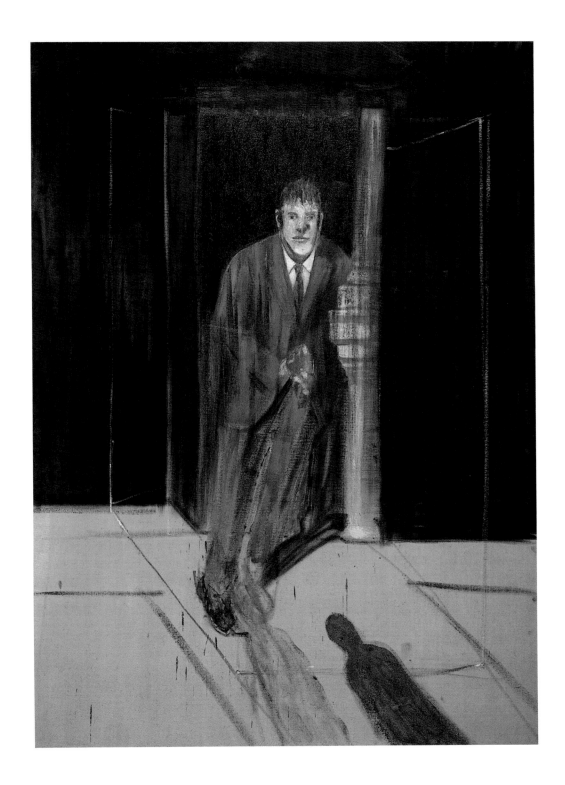

at Munnings and the Royal Academy. He concluded, 'there are, after all, more things in heaven and earth than shiny horses or juicy satins. There are the *fleurs du mal* for instance.'

PAINTING, PHOTOGRAPHY, PORTRAITS, 1951–9

Actually, Michelangelo and Muybridge are mixed up in my mind together.[7]
Francis Bacon, Interview 4, 1974

Bacon's next exhibition at the Hanover in December 1951 included his first portrait with a named subject, *Portrait of Lucian Freud* 1951 (fig.21), derived from a photograph of Franz Kafka. When Freud arrived to pose for Bacon, he found the portrait almost finished with a good likeness. Bacon said he only wanted to work on the feet, but did extensively rework it. Bacon did at times have the subjects of his portraits sit for him. Nevertheless, he would also work from photographs of them or of other things that informed the image he was making.

In 1951–3 Bacon worked in a studio at the Royal College of Art where the *Portrait of Lucian Freud* was painted. The artist Albert Herbert was a student at the time. He recalled in a letter:

> In 1951 John Minton inherited some money and went to Jamaica giving his teaching time to Francis Bacon. Professor Moynihan let Bacon use his studio to work in … I first saw him in the student wash room, stripped to the waist, washing oil paint off his shoulders. I was too shy to comment on this, but at some point I did tell him that oil paint on raw canvas was supposed to rot it. He just shrugged and said 'Degas did it'. He was quite affable and smiley but made no attempt at all to do any teaching … He was not secretive. He left the door of his studio ajar and during his very long lunches I often went in to see what he was doing. There were about 20 canvases, perhaps about 4 x 3 stretched the wrong way round. At one time he filled a bucket with black house paint and with a broom from the corridor splashed it over the canvases. It also went over the walls and ceiling. I noticed that he drew on the canvases with chalk and pastel – working out compositional lines in the traditional way. These lines were eliminated when he painted over

them. He was not quite so spontaneous as he later said. I am certain I remember this correctly because I copied the idea myself.[8]

Painted in the studio Bacon was to occupy, Rodrigo Moynihan's *Portrait Group* 1951 (fig.22) depicts the staff of the Painting School of the Royal College of Art. It is reproduced here to illustrate not only the place and the people with whom Bacon had long lunches but also the contemporary traditionalist painting whose conventions Bacon's paintings were subverting. In some ways he was more academic than they were. He reconfigured the conventions in his evolution from a technically limited painter to a virtuoso in his own pictorial dialect.

The activity of painting deploys skills that come from imitation and practice. Skill is tacit knowledge: capacities grounded in the training of habits of hand and eye. How painters acquire and develop their skills is obviously a fundamental determinant of their work. English art school pedagogy and painting since Ruskin and the Pre-Raphaelites were predominantly linear. Line depicts what we know of the physical structure of things rather than what we see. By the end of the nineteenth century, drawing the nude model was at the core of art school training in Britain.

Bacon lacked this training in a skill rooted in delineating the inert body of the model day in day out for years.

Alternatively, by hue, tone and intensity the painterly approach shows what we see. It is closer to raw sight. In a brief statement in praise of the painter Sir Matthew Smith published in 1953, Bacon advocated a painterly method in which idea and technique were inseparable, in which the 'brushstroke creates the form'. Every movement of the brush on the canvas should alter and shape the image. Paint should never 'merely fill in'.[9] 'Francis said he couldn't draw,' reported the artist Richard Hamilton. 'Maybe what he meant was that he wasn't happy describing the three dimensional object with a line.'[10]

In practice, Bacon keeps both the linear and the painterly in contradictory play. His lines are various, from the ghosts of the initial black drawing to the white lines of the perspective space frames. Black lines might propose the edge of a form otherwise lost in paint. Broken and dotted white lines can evoke a highlight along an edge. In later paintings, he was to add to this vocabulary the undrawn line of nearly raw canvas left between two abutting areas of paint, creating an active border.

23 (left)

Georges Carpentier: 'Carpentier–Bogeyman to British Heavy Weights'; 'Joe Beckett v Georges Carpentier'

Loose leaf from unidentified book on boxing

Oil painting over illustrations

27.5 x 20.8

Tate Archive

24 (right)

Pink Crawling Figure

c.1957–61

Ballpoint pen and oil on paper

40 x 27

Tate

25
Three Studies of the Human Head
1953
Oil on three canvases
Each 61 x 51
Private collection – courtesy Massimo Martino Fine Arts & Projects, Mendrisio

Grounded in the use of photographs, Bacon's skill as an image-maker derived from depictions of bodies in motion. Before the rise of nineteenth-century realism copying the work of others and drawing from statues formed the basis of academic art training. Bacon learnt to draw from copying and working on lens-derived images. The revelation after his death of his works on paper confirms his debt to photography. He drew with a brush and scratched on photographs in a way that summarises posture and movement. In the photograph *Georges Carpentier* (fig.23) Bacon has created a rhythm of brushstrokes down the body. In *Pink Crawling Figure* (fig.24) he uses the brush in the same way to to express movement, here painted over a ballpoint-biro linear drawing.

There are many gestures, postures, facial expressions and bodily movements in Bacon's work that are rare in the work of other painters, even those who use photography. The movement and expression in *Three Studies of the Human Head* 1953 (fig.25) are outside the traditional vocabulary of painting. I cannot think of any other paintings that capture these instant moments of facial movement. The draughtsmanship of the conventionally trained painter carries within it the immobile body, the limited vocabulary of positions and expressions of the inert and bored body of the art school model. Bacon transgressed the habits of educated drawing.

PORTRAYALS

At the core of twentieth-century English traditionalist painting was
a pictorial grammar with rules about how form in space should be
rendered. Such paintings do not just copy an appearance: they use form
and perspective rather as if a landscape painter were to create a contour
map beneath grass, bushes or other elements of a work. A linear sense
of volumetric form in space gives perspectival structure to highlights,
gradations of tone and brush marks. It is the antithesis of photography.
Photographs are mechanical indexes of light and dark upon a surface and

26
Portrait of R.J. Sainsbury
1955
Oil on canvas
115 x 99
Robert and Lisa Sainsbury
Collection, University of
East Anglia, Norwich

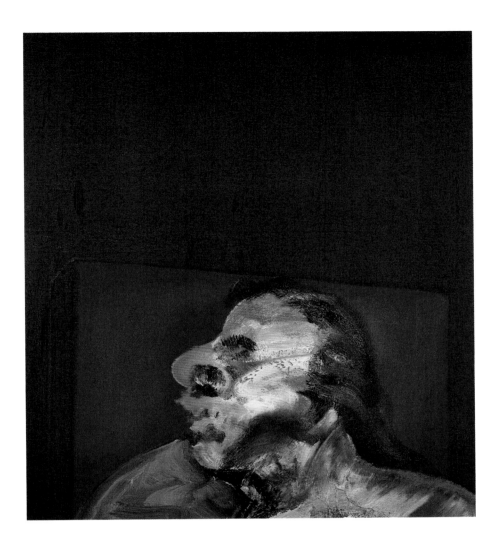

27
Miss Muriel Belcher
1959
Oil on canvas
74 x 67.5
Private collection

are in this sense superficial. Drawing constructs appearances by giving pictorial or plastic structure to them. Bacon's portraits of the early 1950s take this superficiality to an extreme: rather like the Turin Shroud, heads seem to be imprinted onto the canvas, and features onto besuited bodies. At various times he would dab and rub paint on with a cloth, or he might spray, throw or splash it on. The character of his brush marks comes from different sizes of brush. Only occasionally does the movement of Bacon's marks indicate volumetric form. If a shape or structure is implied beneath the painting, it is not that of a linear drawing, but rather the gradations of light as rendered in black and white photography.

Commissioned portraiture was still the economic backbone of many traditionalist painters. In the annual Royal Academy exhibitions of the 1940s to 1960s portraits occupied swathes of wall space. Many of Bacon's paintings were portraits. *Portrait of R.J. Sainsbury* 1955 (fig.26) was commissioned by one of the dynasty of food retailers, who was a major patron of Bacon in the 1950s. One reason that Bacon did not disappear into portraiture in the manner of mainstream English painters was that he did not paint, as they did, as if cinema and photography had never happened.

Bacon continued to paint portraits for the rest of his life. They are some of his most accomplished works. In the period between the mid-1950s and the early 1960s they are perhaps the best of his paintings. *Miss Muriel Belcher* 1959 (fig.27) is one of the paintings where Bacon shifts the emphasis from movement of the human form to movement within the form. Painted into the still of a light green rectangle is an animated head. It is as if we are looking down at someone sleeping on a mattress on the floor. Smears, broken strokes, paint scumbled or textured by dabbing with corduroy, all serve to set up a storm of features. The seemingly closed eyes and the still depths of the greens are the counterpoint to the erupting form. Miss Belcher started the Colony Club in Soho in 1948 with Bacon as a freeloading social attraction. With an endless procession of gin and tonics, she used to perch at the end of the bar next to the door as if she had been there since the Blitz. Each visitor was required to give her a kiss on entry. Bacon painted the portrait from memory when he was in St Ives for three months working for his first exhibition at Marlborough Fine Art.

CRITICAL POLITICS IN THE 1950S

I'm not upset by the fact that people do suffer, because I think the suffering of people and the differences between people are what have made great art, and not egalitarianism.[11]
Francis Bacon, Interview 4, 1974

In the major art critical battles fought by a brilliant generation of writers in Britain in the 1950s Bacon's work was a defining issue. John Berger and David Sylvester were two of the critics. Berger wrote regularly and Sylvester periodically for the influential left-wing *New Statesman*. Susan Sontag pointed out that subscribers to *Readers Digest* were better informed about the Gulag

28
Man in a Cap
c.1945
Oil on board
94 x 73.5
Private collection

and the atrocities of Stalinism than were readers of the *New Statesman*. Berger's politics were close to the pro-Soviet communist party, but he was not a member. In his brand of socialist realism with a human face art should serve the struggle for social justice. Sylvester, however, was concerned with describing the experience offered by a work and its devices, and locating them within art itself, rather than seeing it as an instrument of social and political progress. In 'Curriculum Vitae', the introduction to his collected essays, *About Modern Art: Critical Essays 1948–97*, Sylvester recalls realising at the end of the 1940s that Bacon's work was 'painting, not a cry of pain':

> In the search for figurative art that was new and grand it was important not to be confused by all the retrogressive attempts which a host of painters and sculptors everywhere were making 'to go back to the figure'. Such efforts were insistently promoted by the most influential critic on the scene, John Berger, whose primary heroes were Guttoso, de Staël and Friso ten Holt. It was not surprising that Berger failed to recognise Bacon: he was too much of a boy scout not to see Bacon as a monster of depravity.[12]

Berger wrote about Bacon in the early 1950s. He renewed his critique in an essay 'The Worst Is Not Yet' in 1972, a revised version of which, 'Francis

29
Figure Getting out of a Car
c.1943
Reworked as **Landscape and Car** c.1939–40
Oil on canvas
144.8 x 128.3
Private collection

30 (opposite)
Three Studies for Figures at the Base of a Crucifixion
c.1944 (detail of fig.1)
Oil on three board
Each 94 x 73.7
Tate. Presented by
Eric Hall 1953

Bacon and Walt Disney', was published in 1980 in *About Looking*, an anthology of essays. In this essay he does acknowledge Bacon's achievement, saying 'there has never been painting quite like this'. He refers to his 'mastery', 'his extraordinary skill', 'dedication' and 'lucidity'. He charges Bacon, nevertheless, with being a conformist by acquiescing in the inhumane alienation of modern society: Bacon depicts alienated behaviour and interprets it 'in terms of the worst possible having already happened, and so proposes that both refusal and hope are pointless'. Berger concludes that Bacon's work makes no comment on social relations, on bureaucracy, industrial society or the history of the twentieth century; his work is a demonstration, rather than an expression, of a desire for mindlessness, for absolute alienation.[13]

Writing at a time when ameliorative politics were the common sense of Western governments of both left and right, to describe Bacon's political atheism as 'conformist' was simply untrue. However, Berger's argument has insights. It posits a critical humanism, a claim that humankind is under capitalism alienated from itself, from the product of its creative labour. Life is robbed of meaning. It charges Bacon with offering no hope of a collective redemption from this state of alienation. He is right. For Bacon, how we are is what we are and we are without meaning. This is the human condition. He is a history painter in that he shows us this condition in the twentieth century. The early paintings that are most overtly concerned with current politics he never put forward for public exhibition.

In 1951 Bacon left his studio in Cromwell Place, South Kensington, which was very close to the Victoria and Albert Museum which then housed the Painting School of the Royal College of Art. He sold the lease on to the portrait painter Robert Buhler, who taught at the RCA and was included in Moynihan's *Portrait Group* (fig.22). He found seven abandoned canvases in the studio and sold them; among these was *Man in a Cap* 1941–2 (fig.28). The head in *Man in a Cap* resembles that of the shouting Dr Goebbels recorded in Sam Hunter's photograph of images in Bacon's studio (fig.16). It is one of a million other photographs and films of shouting leaders addressing Nazi and Fascist rallies that invaded the newspapers and newsreels of the 1930s. The body leans its weight onto a rail, and the head is askew of and somehow detached from the anatomical logic of the body, a device that Bacon was to use many times in the future. From the source and context of the photograph we know that the mouth is shouting not screaming, but the physiognomy of the mouth is such that rage, ecstasy and

31

Figure in a Landscape

1945

Oil on canvas

144.8 x 128.3

Tate. Purchased 1950

harangue are indistinguishable in appearance. Bacon's popes are shouting at least as much as they are screaming.

In 1946 a visitor to his studio photographed a painting that Bacon subsequently overpainted (fig.29). The photograph catches an illuminated window and a tray of tea things reflected in the glass of the glazed painting. The origin of the image, Bacon told Ronald Alley, was a photograph of Hitler getting out of a car at one of the Nuremberg rallies.[14] The huge biomorphic monster thrusts its long neck into a bouquet of microphones and flowers. The monster has precedents in both Bacon's earlier work and that of Roy de Maistre. The labial mouth and its exposed teeth reappear in the central panel of *Three Studies for Figures at the Base of a Crucifixion* 1944 (fig.30).

The ghost of a mouth shouting into a microphone can be found in the black that spreads from the open jacket in *Figure in a Landscape* 1945 (fig.31). Its position presupposes the long neck of the biomorphic monster. A snapshot of Bacon's lover and supporter of the 1930s and 1940s, Eric Hall, dozing in a chair in Hyde Park, was the initial source of the painting.

Sigmund Freud used 'over-determined' to describe a symptom, dream image or any other item of behaviour that had more than one meaning or expressed drives and conflicts derived from more than one level or aspect of personality. Bacon channelled into his painting potential meanings as diverse as his pictorial sources. In this sense they are over-determined contrivances. Expressive of images of political power in the twentieth century, the harangue physiognomy continues to figure in his work long after reference to its origin has disappeared. Power as libidinal energy animates Bacon's figures: they are driven by 'some primal, mysterious, sanguinary, self-immolatory craving', to quote again from Isaiah Berlin on Joseph de Maistre.[15]

Berger, in effect, regrets that Bacon has not constructed his practice within ideas of 'social relations', 'bureaucracy', 'industrial society', etc. This is the vocabulary of the enlightenment project, the would-be benign, progressive socio-political overview, a discourse of rational political management and social engineering. Bacon's politics, that is to say his view of power, do not operate within these terms and the historical perspective of progressive intellectuals. Bacon may have become an intellectual, but he had none of their tendency to see themselves and their forms of thought and expertise as having some socially redemptive role.

For Bacon the ahistorical body *in extremis* is the essential actuality in a meaningless world. His sources of conviction are the antithesis to progressive political overviews. Berger is right in that Bacon's work is not a journey into a world of social hope with its critiques of the present. In this respect Berger's description does have insight, but Bacon does not acquiesce in alienation: he asserts it as the brutal and energising primal and ahistorical fact of life. Benignly intended or not, political power is power that rests in essence on organised violence. Bacon's paintings of powerful men recognise this brutal fact and in this they are politically truthful.

32 (opposite left)
Lucian Freud
Francis Bacon
1952
Oil on metal
17.8 x 12.7
Tate. Purchased 1952
Whereabouts unknown

BACON'S MODERNISM AND PICTORIAL SYNTAX

33 (right)
R.B. Kitaj
Synchrony with F B –
General of Hot Desire
1968 (detail)
Oil on two canvases
Each 152.4 x 91.5
Right panel illustrated
Mr and Mrs Ian
Stoutzker, London

One of the reasons why I don't like abstract painting, or why it doesn't interest me, is that I think painting is a duality, and that abstract painting is entirely an aesthetic thing.[16]
Francis Bacon, Interview 2, 1966

Bacon's paintings are unlike the work of the artists thought to be closest to him. In an essay in 1975 the painter R.B. Kitaj coined the phrase 'The School of London', which has come to refer, in particular, to Bacon, Kitaj, Frank Auerbach, Leon Kossoff, Michael Andrews and Lucian Freud, Bacon's onetime friend and ideologically closest companion among these painters.[17] In Freud's work there is a linear and isolating separation of figures from context: in his later work are delineated forms filled with

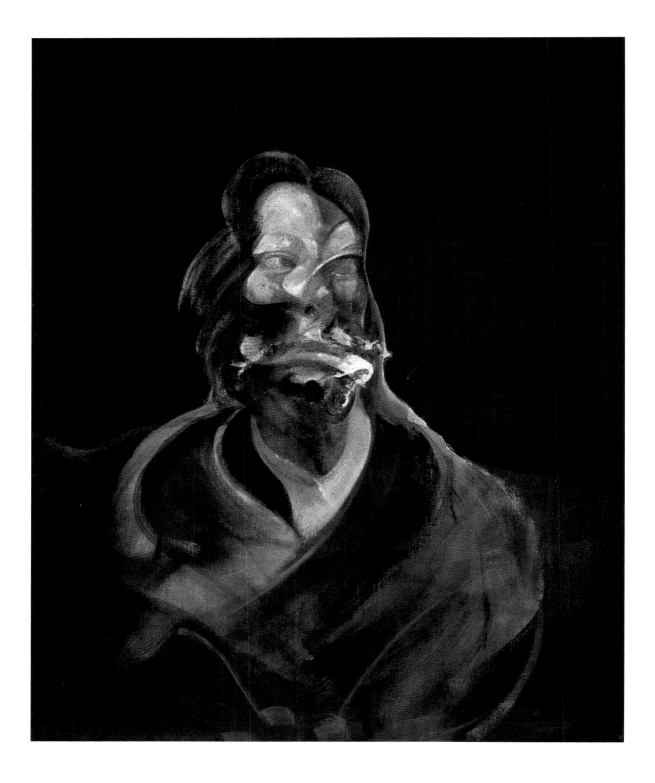

painterly brush work (fig.32). As in Bacon's paintings, light and dark do not meld together to form a shared pictorial space. Only Kitaj has Bacon's diversity of pictorial sources (fig.33). Nevertheless, neither the appearance nor the motivation of work by Kitaj, Freud and the other cited painters could be mistaken for Bacon's. Apart from anything else, they all, even Freud, retain the grammar of art school draughtsmanship in their work.

In the 1975 essay Kitaj argued that an international style was denying just recognition to a school of major figurative painters working in London. Abstract painting, centred on New York, dominated critical and curatorial attention. Clement Greenberg was the most influential theorist and writer of the tendency. Born in New York in 1909, the same year as Bacon, Greenberg provides a point for beginning to locate Bacon's work within the broader terrain of modernist painting and aesthetics.

Mere fashion gives value to paintings that do not manifest anything other than the painter's aesthetic sensations. This was Bacon's dismissive argument about non-figurative painting. In contrast, Greenberg argued that the common characteristic of the most compelling modern art is that it addresses aesthetic sensations particular to its physical medium. Modern painting is about painting to the exclusion of all else, and its highest achievements are predominantly in non-figurative painting.[18]

In Greenberg's terms Bacon was not a modernist. He recognised Bacon's technical debt to academic painting when he observed that Bacon was attempting to make art in the grand manner. In a 1968 interview Greenberg said:

34
Portrait of Isabel
Rawsthorne
1966
Oil on canvas
81.3 x 68.6
Tate. Purchased 1966

> I go for his things at the same time that I see through and around them. It's as though I can watch him putting his pictures together ... I behold the cheapest, coarsest, least felt application of paint matter I can visualize, along with the most transparent, up-to-date devices ... Bacon is the one example in our time of *inspired* safe taste – taste that's inspired in the way in which it searches out the most up-to-date of your 'rehearsed responses.' Some day, if I live long enough, I'll look back on Bacon's art as a precious curiosity of our period.[19]

Greenberg's notion of modernism reconciles art to the tradition of progressive post-enlightenment thought. He saw Immanuel Kant as the first modernist thinker and aesthetician. While Greenberg does not argue for aesthetic progress, he does argue for the progress of aesthetics. Even if past judgements of what was of aesthetic value were often right, modern criticism has, science-like, refuted the grounds given for such opinions. Modernist sensibility arises out of the character of modern thought, out of its ever stricter and narrower requirement for 'the empirical and the positive'. The unified picture plane offers this as an aesthetic experience. It presents aesthetic vivacity without denying the painting's material reality as a flat surface, and it was the essential characteristic of what Greenberg called 'Modernist Painting'.[20]

Bacon's work enacts a different tradition formed in reaction to progressive enlightenment. A ruptured picture plane is the most constant factor in his painting. One part of the painting differs from other parts; there are simultaneously different kinds of pictorial language. Bacon creates explosions of space and movement in and out, across and at angles to the painting's surface, as in *Portrait of Isabel Rawsthorne* 1966 (fig.34). Out of a still darkness an outbreak of painterly marks forms a head and shoulders animated by highlights, dabs of textured paint, splashes of white, transparent strokes over the raw canvas, residual drawing lines and the glance of her right eye. Against this flurry of movement across and arching out of the canvas is the

35
Two Figures
1953
Oil on canvas
152.5 x 116.5
Private collection

36
Eadweard Muybridge
Athletes Wrestling
1887
Photograph
The New York Public Library

stillness of the mouth, the closed left eye and the dark. It is as if a photograph of Rawsthorne is vanishing under a molesting welter of paint.

Bacon chose to have his paintings glazed and because of the reflections and mirroring of the glass it is almost impossible to take in his pictures as a whole. We know the paintings in their entirety from suppressing these effects in our mind's eye and from seeing them in reproduction. (Reproductions suppress disunity in the homogeneity of printer's ink. For instance, a thin indicative brushstroke across raw canvas gains a decisive and integrated plasticity.) Yet, with their energies contained within the great gold frames and the glass, the paintings do offer a kind of totality. Bacon did talk about framing his work with non-reflecting glass but in the thirty or so subsequent years he did not use it. Mistakenly, I think, some public collections have reframed his paintings with glass sans reflection.

The paintings have their roots in a tradition of modernism other than that outlined by Greenberg. 'The ontological view governing the image of man in the work of leading modernist writers,' according to the Marxist literary critic Georg Lukács, is that 'man is by nature solitary, asocial, unable to enter into relationships with other human beings.'[21] Lukács's critique of literary modernism includes discussion of Franz Kafka, James Joyce, Marcel Proust and Samuel Beckett, and refers to T.S. Eliot: all authors whom Bacon read. The bulk of Bacon's paintings depict single figures, a characteristic that is most striking in the distribution of figures between the three separate canvases of the triptychs. Generally, when there is more than one figure in the same canvas they do not share a common space. There are exceptions, the most constant being figures merged in the act of sex: in the primal act they do share pictorial space (fig.35).

Bacon has more in common with and is more indebted to literary modernism than to the pictorial tradition included in Greenberg's account. Greenberg's modernism has its origins in the positive assertion of modernity, in what were often pictorial devices prompted by social and spiritual aspirations, as articulated in the Impressionists' dissolving of weight and abolition of tonal modelling, in the declared materiality and shallow pictorial space of Synthetic Cubism, and in the visual purity and non-figured paintings of Piet Mondrian. These painters painted onto white-primed canvas, while Bacon's stock-in-trade was the mid-toned canvas, in which figured weight, darkness, depth and the animated human form.

4 CRUCIFIXIONS

David Sylvester: *In painting a Crucifixion, do you find you approach the problem in a radically different way from when working on other subjects?* Francis Bacon: *Well, of course, you're working then about your own feelings and sensations, really. You might say it's almost nearer to a self portrait. You are working on all sorts of very private feelings about behaviour and about the way life is.*[1]
Interview 2, May 1966

BACON'S CRUCIFIXIONS are among his most important but not necessarily his most accomplished paintings. They are important and yet less realised because they are often the sites of renegotiations of what he is doing. The repetition of the crucifixion exemplifies one of the characteristics of Bacon's oeuvre, his reworking of motifs. For instance, the series of paintings of popes replays the same basic image with limited variations and additions. However, revisiting the crucifixions could also occasion a fundamental reconsideration, calling into being both new motifs and developments, and setting new technical and aesthetic problems.

PAINTING

37
Painting
1946
Oil and pastel on linen
197.8 x 132.1
The Museum of Modern Art,
New York. Purchase

Painting 1946 (fig.37) is a crucifixion but not named as such. It continues the theme of execution, and compared to the crucifixions of the 1930s it has gained in complexity and pictorial force. It retains traces of the images of Hitler and other leading Nazis, particularly those showing these men on railed podia surrounded by microphones and in open-mouthed harangue. However, this monster has a smudge of yellow that could be a handkerchief in a breast pocket or a Star of David. The idea that the victims of violence can become the perpetrators could have been prompted by contemporaneous Jewish terrorism in Palestine during the final years of the British mandate that ended in 1948. In 1944 Lord Moyne (Walter Guinness), the British Minister Resident in Egypt, was assassinated. This may have engaged Bacon's sympathies as Moyne was an Anglo-Irish Peer who, like Bacon's father, had been a hussar and served in the Boer War.

Railed podia and other confining or space-defining devices reappear in many subsequent works. While the perspective cues within each of Bacon's pictures are mutually contradictory, his figures and perspective do predominantly locate the viewer's eye level about halfway down the painting. We look up at the action in the imaginative space of the painting. For the rest of his working life Bacon returns repeatedly to figures on podia, beds and platforms, like altars raised up from the ground.

In *Painting* 1946, a crucified body hangs like an animal carcass behind the black-robed figure of the open-mouthed executioner. In *Documents* Bataille published photographs of a slaughterhouse, accompanied by a discussion in which he connects religious sacrifice and butchery. The thrust of the text, reports Dawn Ades,[2] is an exposure of the hypocritical and hygienic life of modern man that hides abattoirs from our sight, 'a sign of our inability, in Bataille's view, to tolerate our own ugliness', and in Bacon's words, to face the 'brutality of fact'.

FRAGMENTS OF A CRUCIFIXION AND THE FURIES

The next crucifixion, *Fragments of a Crucifixion* 1950 (fig.38), is a very different and atypical work. Rather than pushing events to the pictorial foreground or mid-ground, the cross is thrust to the literal surface of the painting. The background is a strip of sea and coastline with matchstick figures and cars. Shadowed by companions on either side, a betoothed wide-open mouth within a disproportionately small head and a yet disproportionately smaller body with female pudenda is flapping before the cross. These strange figures are the forebears of the form the Furies take in later paintings.

Bacon refers to the Furies as the Eumenides, the kindly ones, a name given by the Athenians to assuage them. The Furies were the avengers of murder and

38
Fragments of a Crucifixion
1950
Oil and cotton wool on canvas
140 x 108.5
Van Abbemuseum, Eindhoven

39
Three Figures and Portrait
1975
Oil and pastel on canvas
198.1 x 147.3
Tate. Purchased 1977

40
Edgar Degas
After the Bath, Woman Drying Herself 1903
Pastel on paper laid on board
103.5 x 98.5
National Gallery, London.
Bought, 1959

crime against the ties of kinship; they were the personifications of guilt driving their victims to madness. Bacon's depiction of the Furies in *Fragments of a Crucifixion* is closer to the ancient Greek poet Hesiod's description than the form they took in *Three Studies for Figures at the Base of a Crucifixion* (fig.1). Hesiod describes them as three winged women with snakes about them.

Above them in the painting a dog-like creature is draped down from the cross bar. Martin Hammer has suggested that this derives from photographs of Hitler leaning out of windows to touch the outstretched fingers of the adoring crowds.[3] But if we follow Hammer and see the cross as window casements, then the flapping Furies could be falling babies, thrown by the figure above. Accusations of defenestration were in the news with the death of the Czechoslovakian Foreign Minister Jan Masaryk in 1948.

Fragments of a Crucifixion is, as I have said, spatially atypical. The Furies, however, were to revisit Bacon's paintings particularly after the death of his lover George Dyer, for example in *Three Figures and Portrait* 1975 (fig.39). A black-and-white photo-like portrait of Dyer looks down at two convulsing figures in an arena defined by a fractured circular band that moves from flat yellow to shaded rotundity. The figure on the left has the head of Dyer. The spine emerges from its back, an idea derived from Bacon's misreading of a drawing by Degas, *After the Bath, Woman Drying Herself* 1903 (fig.40). Bacon read the roll of flesh and muscle pushed up by the position of the model's scapula as the spine. 'The spine almost comes out of the skin altogether,' he said in 1966. The right-hand figure turns away from the images of Dyer and the viewer. Perched on a box frame in the foreground sits a Fury or perhaps another classical Greek monster, a harpy. Harpies were the souls of the dead in the form of birds with women's faces that snatched the souls of the living. Here the harpy has a fleshy body like an amalgam of buttocks and chickens' thighs with sketchily indicated bird's legs, and a mouth that goes back to the central figure of *Three Studies for Figures at the Base of a Crucifixion* 1944 (fig.30).

THREE STUDIES FOR A CRUCIFIXION

Completed just before his first retrospective at the Tate Gallery in 1962, Bacon's next crucifixion, *Three Studies for a Crucifixion* 1962 (fig.41),

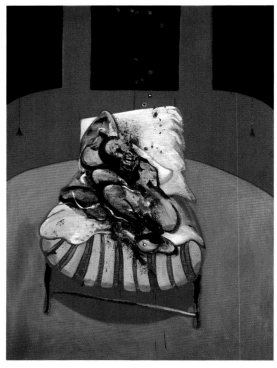

is again an important and predictive transitional work. It was the beginning of the many large and identically sized triptychs he was to make for the rest of his life. David Sylvester in his review of the Tate exhibition for the *New Statesman* argued that since 1957 Bacon had changed from 'treating the canvas as a tank into treating it as a surface'.[4] I do not think this is what Bacon was doing in *Three Studies for a Crucifixion*. Rather than placing his figures in a tank of darkness, he was placing them in rooms. This new flatness was not just the coloured surface of the painting: they are walls. The pictures continue the plane of the floor on which we stand and the rooms are on the other side of the wall. We are placed like spies or police watching events through a one-way mirror.

Sylvester's reference to 1957 points to the paintings that were inaugurated by a series of canvases based on Vincent van Gogh's destroyed *Painter on the Road to Tarascon* 1888 and painted for Bacon's last major exhibition at the Hanover Gallery. In these paintings tone was subordinate to colour. Previously light and dark had described depth and rotundity, and colour

41

Three Studies for a Crucifixion

1962

Oil with sand on three canvases

Each 198.1 x 144.8

Solomon R. Guggenheim Museum, New York

provided incident or emphasis within the tank of darkness. In the van Gogh paintings, rather than describe bodily movement, intense hues laid over each other in explicit brushstrokes created a rhythm across the canvas, emphasising the surface of the painting. Bacon was coming to terms not only with Van Gogh but also, in the wake of the first sightings of American Abstract Expressionism, artists in London were reconsidering colour, paint handling and scale. London had a glimpse of this work in a CIA-backed Museum of Modern Art touring exhibition shown at the Tate Gallery in 1956.

In his 1962 review, Sylvester went on to observe that in the post-1957 work the masses were not linked to the surrounding space. The figure painted onto a separate piece of canvas and then stuck on the main canvas in *Reclining Woman* 1961 (fig.42) makes the point. Furthermore, there is little painterly articulation of the body, which remains a blob of confused and uninteresting hues. Bacon may have been trying to paint the figures as if he was modelling them in coloured clay. He was talking about making sculpture at this time. Sylvester concludes that in *Three Studies for a*

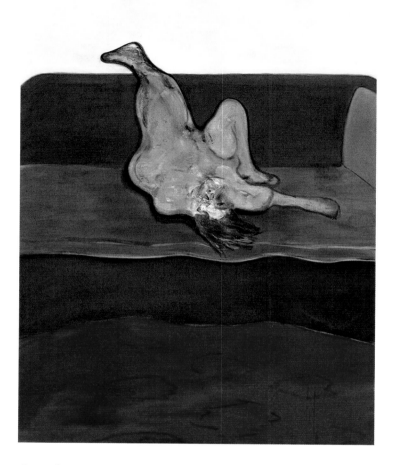

Crucifixion: 'It looks here as if Bacon has been trying to reconcile the compact sculptural character of the forms of his 1944 triptych ... with the more painterly and "realistic" handling of the subsequent work. The space still doesn't entirely convince, but the impact is electrifying all the same.'[5]

Given that the three-canvas format might suggest a story, Bacon was clearly anxious in his comments on the triptych to declare that this was not a narrative. It had been produced under exceptional circumstances over two weeks and he had worked either drunk or severely hung-over, he told Sylvester.[6] At times, he did not know what he was doing. He specifically denied any rational explanation for the figures on the left.

42

Reclining Woman
1961
Oil on canvas
198.8 x 141.6
Tate. Purchased 1961

However, Michael Peppiatt has offered a biographical reading of the painting. He sees the left-hand panel as depicting Bacon's father and Bacon himself in a body stocking or tights with a hint of women's garters and underclothes beneath. It is the moment of Bacon's expulsion from home. In the centre canvas Peppiatt recognises the bed as Bacon's bed from Morocco upon which he received many beatings from his lover Peter Lacey and others as part of masochistic sex. At the time of painting Lacey was dying in Morocco. The inverted figure on the right, Bacon revealed, came from a crucifix by the thirteenth-century Florentine painter Cimabue that suggested to him a worm crawling down the cross. Peppiatt sees this as an example of the sublimation of personal pain in a universal symbol.[7]

Against Peppiatt's biographical reading, in the culminating chapter of *Francis Bacon and Nazi Propoganda*, Martin Hammer offers a very different account. He is able to bring his exploration of Bacon's use of Nazi graphics as a source to argue the painting as 'infused with recollections of photographic imagery associated in various ways with the period around the war'. He finds sources for the setting in the triptych, as he does in earlier work including *Three Studies for Figures at the Base of a Crucifixion* (fig.1), in photographs of Nazi architecture. He is able to quote Bacon as having said, even if he did then deny having said it, that the standing figures in the left panel were 'Himmler and Hitler opening the doors of the gas chamber'. He suggests resemblances between the two figures and photographs of Hitler and Himmler. The black curved rectangle and square are possibly derived from photographs of the crematorium at Auschwitz and the orange receding rectangle on the left the trolley used to carry bodies for mass burning.

The painting has the rawness of a transitional work, transitional not only in the formal sense that Sylvester argued but also in the use of autobiographical incidents as a source. The painting's failure arises from the forcing of this new content. The two figures on the left hang indecisively in the space of the picture. The central figure has areas of animated painting, but in its disorder it becomes illustrative. Paint ceases to describe movement, becoming unambiguously blood, torn flesh and exposed teeth. The lack of clarity of much of the right-hand figure seems arbitrary within the easily recognised horror. It lacks painterly life.

The biographical reading suggests that the painting is an announcement of enraged grief or, less sympathetically, dramatised self-pity. The picture is a massed assault by hue, imagery and title. With no cross the Christian connotations come from Bacon's choice of title. There is blasphemy in the snarl of the ape-like teeth of the inverted body derived from an image of Christ. As the last painting in his first retrospective in the Tate Gallery, there could hardly be a more offensive image. This painting, or at least its reference to Cimabue, provoked the renegade Christian art critic Peter Fuller to describe Bacon as an 'evil genius' and to condemn his vision of humankind as 'odious'.[8]

43
Crucifixion
1965
Oil on three canvases
Each 198 x 147.5
Bayerische Staatsgemälde-
sammlungen Pinakothek der
Morderne, Munich

AUTOBIOGRAPHY AND *CRUCIFIXION*

Bacon was to return to similar motifs two years later in another triptych, *Crucifixion* 1965 (fig.43). Apart from the new version of *Three Studies for Figures at the Base of a Crucifixion* produced in 1988, it was the last painting he was to call a crucifixion. Again there is the mangled figure on the bed, this time in the left canvas and observed at a distance by a naked

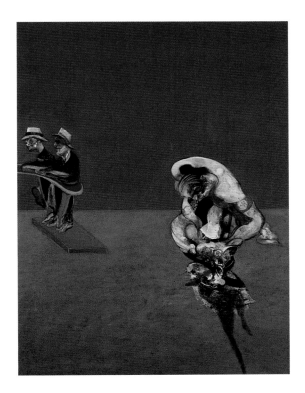

woman. Is this a return to autobiography, but with the mother's indifference as the personal wound? In her deformities she is the pictorial sister of the female figure in *After Muybridge – Study of the Human Figure in Motion – Woman Emptying a Bowl of Water/Paralytic Child Walking on all Fours* (fig.3). This was painted in the same year, and I have already suggested that the painting has an autobiographical source. Here again is the opened-up and upturned figure, this time in the middle panel, with bound arms and within its entrails the suggestion of a bird, which in later paintings converges with the depiction of the Furies. On the right two men in Panama hats are leaning against some surface that could be anything from racetrack fencing to a bar. Moreover, in the foreground a figure described by Michel Leiris, the French writer and friend of Bacon, as 'a man, scarcely visible except for his tricolour cockade, is being molested by someone wearing a swastika armband'.[9] Given the position of the dominated figure and the dash of red there is a suggestion of bloody fellatio. In this reading the figure is an explicit image of an implicit theme that runs through Bacon's work: the eroticism of sex, violence and political power.

In one of his interviews Sylvester reported to Bacon that people thought the figure was either a Nazi or the character dressed as a Nazi in Genet's play *The Balcony*.[10] He suggested this was an example of people making a narrative interpretation. Bacon said he disliked such interpretations. The swastika had no motive other than a need for a patch of red. Nevertheless, there is another narrative cue or link. Both the figure on the bed and the figure Leiris describes on the right have tricolour cockades.

I think the 1962 and 1965 triptychs fail to convince as paintings. They are too literal attempts at the same subject in which personal and recent violent history are conjoined. *Three Studies for a Crucifixion* 1962 and *Crucifixion* 1965, like *Painting* 1946 and *Fragments of a Crucifixion* 1950, renegotiated what Bacon's work was about. They made new technical demands that later paintings were to meet. They were in terms of his developing ambition some of Bacon's most important and revealing paintings. To return to scenes of human sacrifice as a given of life and history was to revisit a core motif in, and motivation for, his work. But in reviving the crucifixion motif, he came close to, and I think fell into, the sin of illustration. They illustrate what Bacon thought his work was about.

5 ILLUSTRATION AND THE DYER TRIPTYCHS

I think in our previous discussions, when we've talked about the possibility of making appearance out of something which is not illustration, I've over-talked about it. Because, in spite of theoretically longing for the image to be made of irrational marks, inevitably illustration has to come into it.[1]
Francis Bacon, Interview 5, 1975

ILLUSTRATION IS A KEYSTONE term in the structure of Bacon's discussion of his own work. From his earliest to last statements, he used it repeatedly to indicate what his work was not. His idea of what he was doing revolved around distinguishing it from illustration. In citing illustration as the antithesis to art he was not alone.

For Clement Greenberg illustration accompanies another term of disparagement relevant to Bacon: 'literary'. Whereas, for instance, Bacon admired Picasso's work when he was close to the Surrealists, between 1926 and 1932, for Greenberg this was when Picasso lost his way in 'illustrative expressionism'. In *The Three Dancers* 1925 (fig.13), the painting in which Picasso announced his semi-detached alignment with the Surrealists and to which I have already referred as a source for Bacon, Picasso becomes illustrative and literary, argues Greenberg:

> Now illustration addresses nature, not in order to make art say something through nature, but in order to make nature itself say something – and say it loudly. Yet the *Three Dancers* goes wrong, not just because it is literary (which is what making nature speak through art comes to), but because the theatrical placing and rendering of the

head and arms of the centre figure cause the upper half of the picture to wobble. (Literature as such has never yet hurt a work of pictorial art; it is only literary *forcing* that does that.)[2]

Seen in these terms, Bacon's work is illustration. It does make nature, often horrifically fractured, speak through art and loudly. What then did Bacon mean by illustration?

Bacon seems to have thought that illustration comes in two forms: images that are subordinate to a text, that is, they illustrate words; and images that merely imitate appearances. He gives an example of the latter when he claims that for him photography is always illustration. The clearest example he gives of not-illustration is a disputed Rembrandt, *Self-Portrait* c.1659 (fig.44). 'There is a coagulation of non-representational marks which have led to making up this very great image,' said Bacon. A counter-example of a merely representational painting might be the later work of Graham Sutherland (fig.45), which Bacon, in a final break with his former supporter and friend, likened to a *Time* magazine cover. What such paintings fail to do, in Bacon's terms, is to have a direct effect upon the viewer's 'nervous system'.

It is around Bacon's distinction between illustration and paintings as art that the French philosopher Giles Deleuze (1925–1995) in his book *Francis Bacon: Logique de la Sensation* (1981) conducts his discussion of Bacon's paintings.[3] Deleuze offers a complex of distinctions between painting as art (the figure) and illustration (the figurative) to argue Bacon's work as essentially aggregates of the visual sensations of enfleshed being. However, it asks us to ignore or demote that in Bacon's work that is dependent on figurative recognition, such as the directional force of a figure's glance or the recognisable face of a person. More broadly, it denies the linear when it works with the recognition of things rather than the optical sensation of the painterly. These are core characteristics of Bacon's paintings, which function by their non-resolution of illustration and painting as art.

In their non-resolution Bacon's paintings are an incitement to interpretation. It is a mistake to accept Bacon's denials of linguistic sources and intent. As Paul Valéry, one of the authors he admired, argued, 'all the arts live by words. May not the prime motive of any work be the wish to give rise to discussion, if only between the mind and itself?'[4] The operative word here is discussion, which implies an exchange without conclusion. Contrived as an

44

Rembrandt van Rijn

Self-Portrait

c.1659

Oil on canvas

30 x 24

Musée Granet,

Aix-en-Provence

45

Graham Sutherland

Somerset Maugham

1949

Oil on canvas

137.2 x 63.5

Tate. Presented by Lady

John Hope 1951

incitement to words, Bacon's images call for and refuse description. As Ernst van Alphen shows in the first chapter of his book, *Francis Bacon and the Loss of Self*, 'his works cancel out, as well as stimulate narrative readings'.[5]

THE DYER TRIPTYCHS

How does the left panel from *Triptych – In Memory of George Dyer* 1971 (fig.46) work as both incitement and resistance to words? On a great flat pink wall at about eye level there is an eruption of smeared and brushed paint, a figure crouched or fallen on what could be a shelf or bench (possibly a cushioned bar bench); either his shin is missing or it disappears into the cushion. The 'or' and 'could be' are vital, for in them lies the virulence of the image. The figure is a suggestive mess of internal contradictions. It grabs the attention like a guilty glimpse of a human freak or a bloody accident. Dressed like a boxer, the figure has one foot bootless. The left arm sweeps into rotundity in a highlight on flesh pink and ends in a fist as if delivering an uppercut. The right arm is merely signalled by a black outline among the general suggestion of

thoracic musculature. The head either pulls the foreshortened perspective of the body around towards us or is dislocated. The eyes look up like a supplicant dog. So it goes on.

In other words, the painting stimulates our knowledge of the human body. It calls forth acts of instantaneous recognition below the level of thought comparable to our spontaneous actions when encountering people in the street, actions that answer such unspoken questions as: who is it, do they threaten me, do I desire them? Disruption brings these habitual reflexes into consciousness. Bacon sets up expectations of norms and fears of abnormalities. To refer back to Greenberg's argument (p.75–6), the paintings threaten nature speaking virulently through art, as does a photograph of some human freak or wound. Bacon collected and painted on photographs of such things. The instant horror, revulsion and fascination of these images attest that at some level we do experience them as if real. It would seem that to the 'nervous system' the distinction between 'that looks like' and 'that is' is frail. We recognise the human form with a particular virulence. Deleuze symptomizes the 'lingusistic turn' in theorised writing about art. For its own coherence it minimises the difference between signs that work by recognition of a resemblance and phonemes that are arbitrary signs comprehended in a lingusistic system. It talks as if the image of a face works in much the same way as the word 'face'. Horrific nature is imminent within the ambiguity of fractured pictorial conventions. In the 1971 *Triptych* panel, for instance, this is evident in the shifts from the linear to the painterly, such as the cartoon-like clarity of the boot and leg conjoined with the ambiguities of the thorax. The image incites a perceptual panic, a need to make sense, to conceptualise and to recognise. Nevertheless, it refuses to satisfy those needs unambiguously. Asked what does that depict, we might reply without thinking, 'it looks like a fallen boxer', but know that it is only the start of a discussion. It offers no common sense unification of the faculties, but nor is it Deleuze's recognition-free sensation. It is the faculties in confusion.

The danger of representation in painting is that it is both illustrative and narrative. Realist images incite realist texts, prose in which events are part of a sequence, a narrative or some other form of what Bacon called a 'diatribe through the brain'.[6] Fractured representation, broken realism and disrupted illustration incite meanings in which narrative cannot function, and interpretation and common sense do not rule.

Biographical narrative threatens the paintings inaugurated by the death of George Dyer, who died alone, full of booze and pills, sitting on the lavatory

48
Triptych May–June 1973
1973
Oil on three canvases
Each 198 x 147.5
Private collection

49

**Triptych – In Memory
of George Dyer**

1971

Oil on three canvases

Each 198 x 147.5

Fondation Beyeler,

Reihen/Basel

in their hotel room in Paris. Bacon told, with variations, the story of Dyer, the handsome uneducated petty criminal with a speech impediment he met in 1964; Dyer became his lover and drank himself to death on Bacon's money. His biographers have repeated the story, and it is the subject of the feature film by John Maybury, *Love is the Devil*, released in 1998. After Dyer's death in 1971 Bacon returned to Dyer's image repeatedly over the next four years. He is the subject of three triptychs, is portrayed in a fourth and appears in a number of other paintings.

Dyer's death is shown in *Triptych May–June 1973* (fig.48). A number of devices prevent the work from becoming like a cartoon strip. Dyer expires in the first frame in a conventional left to right narrative reading. The changing furniture of the black space further interrupts narrative continuity: a lavatory, a light bulb and then a sink. On the left and right panels the light switches are on different sides of the door. Arbitrarily, two arrows suggest the diagrammatic, as if this is a how-to-do-it illustration.

Is *Triptych – In Memory of George Dyer* 1971 (fig.49) an autobiographical illustration? To refuse to recognise Dyer would be like refusing to recognise Rembrandt in his self-portraits or Marat in Jacques-Louis David's *Death of Marat* 1793 (Royal Museums of Fine Arts Belgium). The crouched/

fallen figure in the left canvas and in the right is perhaps Dyer, and Dyer's reflection spills over a table. The profile, down to the slick of hair at the back of his head, comes from a photograph of Dyer by John Deakin (fig.50). The central canvas is one of the most architecturally depicted spaces in all of Bacon's paintings. Dyer's shadow-like profile sits on the surface of the panel, disrupting spatial coherence. Picasso uses the same device in the top right of *The Three Dancers* (fig.51; one source of the wobble Greenberg deprecates in the painting). There are other spatial destabilising devices, the slant of the window, for instance, and the break in the door's receding perspective caused by the perfect circle of the Yale lock on the surface of the canvas. The arm that feeds the key into the lock traverses the back of the man at the door like the serpents in the first-century-AD statue of the sea monsters crushing Laocoön and his sons to death (*Laocoön and his Two Sons*, Vatican Museum, Rome).

Disrupting immanent realism saves the paintings from illustration, from storytelling. Bacon's paintings work by the threat of illustration and by its disarrangement. In the words of the Russian Formalist critic, Roman Jakobson, modern literature is a kind of writing that represents an 'organised violence committed on ordinary speech'.[7] To enact its violence, literature needs ordinary speech. The paintings of Francis Bacon need illustration, or the figurative, for they aspire to the condition of modernist literature.

50
John Deakin
Portrait of George Dyer
c.1964
Gelatin silver print mounted
on cardboard, found in
Francis Bacon's studio
The Estate of Francis Bacon

51
Pablo Picasso
The Three Dancers
1925 (detail of fig.13)
Oil on canvas
215.3 x 142.2
Tate

6 ERIC HALL AND THE POETS

I always feel I've been influenced by Eliot. The Waste Land *especially and the poems before it have always affected me very much.*[1]
Francis Bacon, Interview 6, 1979

THAT ARM FEEDING THE KEY into the lock in *Triptych* 1971 is a motif Bacon had used before and was to use again. It alludes, Bacon said, to lines from T.S. Eliot's *The Waste Land*, first published in 1922:

> I have heard the key
> Turn in the door once and turn once only
> We think of the key, each in his prison
> Thinking of the key, each confirms the prison

In a corroboration of Georg Lukács's characterisation of the ontology of literary modernism quoted earlier (p.61), Eliot in his 'Notes' on *The Waste Land* appends a quotation from philosopher F.H. Bradley:

> My experience falls within my own circle, a circle closed on the outside; and, with all its elements alike, every sphere is opaque to the others that surround it … In brief, regarded as an existence which appears in a soul, the whole world for each is peculiar and private to that soul.[2]

For Bradley it is impossible for two minds to know the world in the same way. The world is an interdependent whole, but, as we cannot know it in its totality, our acts of comprehension are inescapably partial. Language is a broken tool: between it and that of which it speaks falls the shadow of an unfathomable disjunction. Thus, in isolation we reach out to each other with the defective tools of language.[3] Given the central importance of the poem to Bacon, it is perhaps not too wilful to see his space frames as a realisation of the closed circle, a space unique and inescapable.

ERIC HALL

The poets Bacon mentions in the Sylvester interviews are of Eric Hall's generation not of Bacon's. Hall was fifteen years older than Bacon, wealthy, a patron of the arts, an Epicurean and possessor of the classical education that Bacon, who regretted that he was unable to read ancient Greek, felt he lacked. Hall was at Malvern School and then went up to Trinity College, Oxford, in 1909, to read classics though he left without graduating. The dominant philosophical figure at Oxford at that time was F.H. Bradley. T.S. Eliot came to England to study his work there in 1914. Perhaps Hall picked up something of the ideas of arguably the most fundamental influence on Eliot's world-view. He was a Captain in the Middlesex Regiment in the First World War, was wounded and a prisoner of war. In 1931 he was elected to the London County Council (LCC) as a member of the Municipal Reform Party and made an Alderman. The Municipal Reform Party was the Conservative Party by another name; they were critics of public expenditure and anti-Socialist. He was a lay magistrate and after the Second World War deputy chairman of the LCC.

Hall wrote letters to the *Times* and his views are reported in accounts of LCC debates. In 1933 the *Times* published his letter criticising the Home Office for the number of Jews of Polish and German origin who were being admitted into the UK. While 'our stock has been greatly enriched in the past by our traditional policy of offering refuge to Jews', the current refugees were destitute and undesirable people 'who have associated themselves with extreme Communist organisation in Germany'. Having responsibility for the administration of Public Assistance in the East End he had 'sympathy for exiled Jews but a greater consideration at this time for our own harassed ratepayers and taxpayers'.[4] He criticised the Labour controlled LCC for ending Army Cadet Training in schools, for not applying to Communists the ban on Fascists using LCC school halls for their meetings and he supported voluntary sterilisation for mental patients. He was critical of the extension of compulsory education to over twelve-year-olds but advocated technical rather than academic education for working-class teenagers. He raised concerns that every effort should be taken to preserve Jacob Epstein's sculpture that was to be removed from Rhodesia House. The LCC had no powers in the matter and it was destroyed. Hall in the context of his time was very clearly a man of the Right but not of the Fascist right. Bacon's use of Fascist images explored by Martin Hammer raises the question of his politics in the 1930s. On the evidence of Hall's politics and their close relationship there are no grounds for thinking Bacon had Fascist sympathies.

Hall was of immense help to Bacon. He bought his work and introduced him to good food, wine, music and theatre, gave him an entrée into cultivated circles, arranged exhibitions that included Bacon's work and defended it in print. Hall left his wife and family to live with Bacon in 1936. He and Bacon travelled widely in Europe during the 1930s. Their relationship ended in the early 1950s. He was to die living alone at his London Club leaving at today's value nearly a million pounds. Like Roy de Maistre, Hall became a Christian, but an Anglican not a Catholic. 'Of late he could be seen in the afternoon walking to evensong at Westminster Abbey,' reported his brief *Times* obituary of 20 October 1959.

In part thanks to Hall, Bacon's social milieu in the 1930s was an upper-class, educated – meaning at that time with an education grounded in Greek and Latin – and culturally advanced bohemia. He went on to mix with the circle around *Horizon*. To be a culturally competent participant in such company would require familiarity with a shared body of reading. Freud, T.S. Eliot and the poets Bacon cites would be *de rigeur*.

POETS AS MODELS

In 1945 Hall bought *Three Studies for Figures at the Base of a Crucifixion* c.1944 (fig.1), which he presented in 1953, as he did other works, to the Tate Gallery. This work, as has been said, was in part derived from reading Aeschylus, but read in the light of William Bedell Stanford's *Aeschylus in his Style: A Study in Language and Personality*, published in 1942. Stanford was one of the contributors to the scholarly critique of the Greeks as English gentlemen, the 'sweetness and light' interpretation of classical culture. The character of his translation of certain passages, for instance 'The reek of human blood smiles out at me', is specifically connected by Sylvester to the painting.[5] However, the influence of this book may have gone beyond the translations it offered. The characterisation of Aeschylus and the discussion of his borrowing from colloquial forms and medical terms as well as from past literature, all present a model of the poet that foreshadows Bacon's work and its multiple sources. Stanford's summary of antiquity's view of Aeschylus can be translated into a description of Bacon and his painting:

> Archaistic yet self-willed and individualistic; contemptuous of popular taste; careless of poetic technique; having a noticeably 'architectural' quality; using a weighty diction that verges on pomposity; obscure; fond of long, strange, and astonishing words; prone to unevenness and incoherence; using harsh-sounding phrases and scorning euphonic devices; with daring imagery sometimes bordering on the grotesque.[6]

The importance of Eliot and Ezra Pound for Bacon is in part, likewise, as models of how to be an artist. What distinguished art from other things, how to relate to past art and present culture, to these and other questions their poetry and criticism provided indicative answers that could be translated, but not transcribed, into pictorial practice.

Bacon was a maker of images. He speaks often of making images rather than of making paintings. He wanted the images to assault 'the nervous system', to have an instantaneous effect. 'An "Image" is that which presents an intellectual and emotional idea complex in an instant of time,' wrote Pound, and it is beyond the 'word formulated in language'.[7] In addition, he was to say in his essay on Henri Gaudier-Brzeska, 'an image is real because we know it directly'. Bacon was an Imagist, to use a flag under which Pound briefly sailed.

Bacon's motifs and the way he worked them resemble those of the poets he admired. Like Pound and Eliot, Bacon reworks classical themes, most conspicuously the Furies from Aeschylus's *Oresteia* as portrayed in Stanford's commentary. His use of past art resembles Eliot's and Pound's quotes from and allusions to past literature and his use of photography equates to their employment of demotic speech. Rather than some Romantic, Expressionist or indeed Surrealist idea of spontaneous expression, Bacon's appropriation of past art enacts Eliot's and Pound's insistence on poetry as an acquired art, an art of structure informed by the peaks and techniques of past literature.

Eliot's much-cited essay, 'Tradition and the Individual Talent', from the collection *The Sacred Wood*, appeared in 1920. The most famous passage reads: 'The more perfect the artist, the more completely separate in him will be the man who suffers and the mind that creates; the more perfectly will the mind digest and transmute the passions which are its material.'[8] Bacon referred to but misunderstood the passage. He understood it to say 'life had nothing to do with art. But I always think he was wrong in a way about that'.[9] Bacon missed the significance of the word 'transmute', to change the form of one thing into another, to change life into art.

Investigating Bacon's pictorial and ideological sources tells us something of what, and the ways in which, he transmuted. They do not tell us why the paintings are still vivid and charismatic. Suppress your knowledge of his work in reproduction; look at the paintings. They are difficult to see and grasp. They thrive on the viewer's insecurity, on the imperfection of transmutation, on the uncertain boundary between illustration and the painterly. They are stylistically unresolved. They refuse any one mode of attention. You can see the kinetic movement of brush or splash, which like abstract expressionist painting articulates a rhythm in pictorial space. Space is also articulated in the Mannerist drama of a figure's direction of glance, its movement, gestures and strain, as in a Michelangelo drawing. There are variegated lines, which come and go, change hue and thickness. They can describe the boundaries of forms, as in Degas, or establish an independent spatial life, as in Cubism. Photography-like chiaroscuro gives the protuberance of a mouth or rotundity of a lip. Van Gogh-broken orange and white hues are conjoined with Rembrandt-dark to give flesh that abuses the logic of skeleton or skull. New York School fields of colour are substantiated into an architecture of walls, walls that can invade the body. The body's ectoplasmic shadows can, as in Picasso, block out walls and their architectural logic. All this assaultive disparity goes on behind reflective glass in pompous gold frames appropriate for an English country house. These painting are both avant-garde and kitsch.

'Some day, if I live long enough, I'll look back on Bacon's art as a precious curiosity of our period' said Clement Greenberg. He is vindicated in that Bacon's work demands to be valued in ways peculiar to itself. However, few artists' work of the second half of the twentieth century will tell the future as much as Bacon's paintings do about their period. They will tell something of our disenchantment and fear.

7 BACON'S DELAY

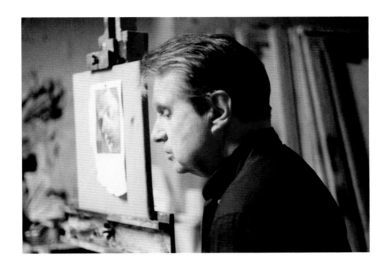

52 (opposite)
Portrait of John Edwards
1988
Oil on canvas
198 x 147.5
The Estate of Francis Bacon

ON EASTER SATURDAY 1992 Francis Bacon flew to Madrid where he was to die five days later. Barry Joule drove him to the airport. Joule, a Canadian of independent means with a science background, was a neighbour of Bacon's, and since 1978 he had become a friend (fig.53). He was interested in Bacon and art, and it was, recalls Joule, a pupil/teacher relationship. Bacon did not drive, so Joule drove Bacon around London and on trips to continental Europe. He helped the increasingly infirm Bacon with practical tasks in his flat and studio, including destroying rejected paintings. Bacon, says Joule, was always very precise with his instructions for the destruction of his works.[1]

53
Barry Joule
Portrait of Francis Bacon
1982
Bacon photographed in
1982 standing next to
a photograph of himself
taken by Helmar Lerski
in Berlin in 1928

On the morning of his departure Joule arrived to drive Bacon to Heathrow. Bacon handed him an old photograph album; a ribbon held it and its contents together. On the way to the airport Joule asked Bacon what he wanted him to do with the album. Bacon used a phrase he had used before when making a gift, 'you know what to do with it'. Bacon had removed the family snaps and filled the album with drawings in oil, often on collaged photographs. Four years later Joule started to make the work public by approaching various Bacon scholars and institutions. The emergence of this album and, from other sources, works on paper and previously unknown paintings put the predominant understanding of Bacon into question.

Apart from Picasso, one of the few twentieth-century artists for whom Bacon consistently declared admiration was Marcel Duchamp. Claiming to have given up making art, Duchamp kept secret the final work of his life, *Etant Donnés*. Its appearance in 1969 after his death disrupted the whole understanding of Duchamp. In an essay discussed by Bacon and Sylvester in one of the interviews Duchamp argued that art ceases to be art when the creative work of the spectator is over and the work's meanings and value have become established.[2] A work, Duchamp estimated, is art for only about twenty years. The appearance of Bacon's works on paper – sketches and drawings in oil paint, biro and pencil on paper, pages of books and photographs – disrupted the established accounts of Bacon. They change the history of the conception and execution of the paintings. There is now a new body of sources for his images. What is the aesthetic and monetary value of the works on paper? How do they relate to his other work? Are they all authentic? If he dissembled about his drawings, what else did he lie about? Bacon scholarship is still raw.

In the summer of 1999 an exhibition *Francis Bacon: Paintings from the Estate 1980–1991* was held in the second floor gallery of Faggionato Fine Art in Albermarle Street, London. The building overlooks the frontage of Marlborough Fine Art on the opposite side of the road. Shortly after Bacon joined Marlborough in 1958, they moved to a new gallery in Bond Street. With their growing success, Marlborough bought and built their way through the block and eventually opened a frontage on the Albermarle side. At the same time Marlborough was making partnerships and opening galleries in Rome, New York and Zurich, in all of which Bacon was to have one-person exhibitions. In the same period that Bacon left the Hanover for Marlborough other artists, including Henry Moore, Barbara Hepworth, Ben Nicholson and Graham Sutherland, were leaving the galleries who had been promoting and selling their work for years and joined Marlborough. Marlborough offered to look after the day-to-day administration of the artists' affairs and provide a new level of international promotion, regular stipends and higher prices, of which the artist would usually get fifty per cent. Bacon gave the size of his debts and the lack of sympathy of Erica Brausen's backers for his work as his reasons for leaving the Hanover Gallery.

Exhibitions in and purchases by prestigious art museums are primary indicators of an artist's reputation and future value. Marlborough built their reputation and that of their artists by putting on museum-like exhibitions in the gallery with catalogues modelled on those of the Museum of Modern Art in New York. They targeted museums as buyers for their artists' work. One marketing device was to arrange an exhibition in a museum as if it was a curatorially independent selection. In fact, Marlborough owned much of the work in these exhibitions. Thus, prestige and value accrued to the gallery's holdings. Lee Seldes in her book *The Legacy of Mark Rothko: An Exposé of the Greatest Art Scandal of Our Century* cites a Bacon exhibition as an example.[3] She claims that the exhibition held at the Metropolitan Museum, New York, in 1975 consisted, with only three exceptions, of Marlborough-owned works. 'Your Gallery has never looked better,' one dealer is said to have remarked to Frank Lloyd, the co-founder of Marlborough, at the opening. 'Is the art market something that you dislike?' Bacon was asked in an interview. 'No, not particularly,' was his reply.[4]

The Faggionato exhibition of 1999 included *Portrait of John Edwards* 1988 (fig. 52). The painting echoes the posthumous paintings of George Dyer, but there are no virulent disruptions. The space in the painting is unbroken and perspectively coherent. The flesh-coloured shadow suggests no monsters of guilt. It is an old man's celebration of a young man made in the residue of a way of painting prompted by very different motives, and is one of many portraits of Edwards. Bacon had met him in 1974 when for a time Bacon had owned a house in the East End of London. Their relationship endured and was essentially paternal. It was to Edwards that Bacon left his estate, then valued at more than £11 million. The relationship between the estate and Marlborough broke down, and the gallery end of the management of the estate passed to a New York dealer, Tony Shafrazi, and Faggionato Fine Art in London.

Bacon's closing years, wrote Sylvester, 'were lightened by the society of a young, good-looking, cultivated Spaniard'.[5] Joule describes the relationship as tempestuous. He travelled to Madrid in his last days to rekindle this friendship with José Capéllo but died there of a heart attack on 28 April 1992, nursed by two nuns of the Servants of Mary.

NOTES

INTRODUCTION

1 Plato, *Republic*, 353D, as rendered in Bernard Williams, *Ethic and the Limits of Philosophy*, London 2006, p.1.

PRETEXTS FOR DESPAIR

1 David Sylvester, *Interviews with Francis Bacon 1962–1979*, London 1997a, p.133.
2 Michael Peppiatt, *Francis Bacon: Anatomy of an Enigma*, London 1996, p.103.
3 Sylvester 1997a, p.83.
4 David Sylvester, Bacon Interviews, 23 April 1975, transcript, Tate Archive, p.26.
5 David Canadine, *The Decline and Fall of the British Aristocracy*, New Haven and London 1990, p.272.
6 Ronald Alley and John Rothenstein, *Francis Bacon*, London 1964.
7 John Russell, *Francis Bacon*, London 1971.
8 Sigmund Freud, 'The Economic Problems of Masochism', in *On Metapsychology*, The Penguin Freud Library Volume II, London 1991, p.424.
9 David Sylvester, *Francis Bacon: The Human Body*, exh. cat., Hayward Gallery, London 1998, p.95.
10 Quoted in Peppiatt 1996, p.29.
11 Ibid., p.27.
12 Patrick White, *Flaws in the Glass: A Self-Portrait*, London, 1998, p.62.
13 Sylvester 1997a, p.59.
14 Peppiatt 1996, p.27.

IDEOLOGIES OF DESPAIR

1 David Sylvester, Bacon Interviews, 23 April 1975, transcript, Tate Archive, p.13.
2 Herbert Read, *Art Now*, London 1933, p.144.
3 Maynard Keynes, 'The Arts Council, its Policy and Hopes', *The Listener*, 12 July 1945.
4 Barry Joule, 'Francis Bacon: A Brief Memoir', in *The Barry Joule Archive: Works on Paper Attributed to Francis Bacon*, exh. cat., Irish Museum of Modern Art, Dublin 2000, p.8.
5 Russell 1971, p.6.
6 Betty Macmurray, Memoir, unpublished Ms in private hands.
7 David Ward, *Patrick White: A Life*, London 1991, p.149.
8 Heather Johnson, *Roy de Maistre: The English Years 1930–1968*, Rosevill East, NSW 1995, p.28.
9 John Rothenstein, 'Introduction', in *Roy de Maistre: A Retrospective Exhibition of Paintings and Drawings 1917–1960*, exh. cat., Whitechapel Art Gallery, London 1960, p.8.
10 Ward 1991, p.174.
11 Isaiah Berlin, 'The Hedgehog and the Fox', in *Russian Thinkers*, ed. Henry Hardy and Aileen Kelly, Harmondsworth 1979, p.60.
12 Hon. William Gibson, *The Abe de Lammenais and the Liberal Catholic Movement in France*, London 1896.
13 T.S. Eliot, 'Introduction', in Charles Baudelaire, *Intimate Journals*, trans. Christopher Isherwood, London 1989, pp.xviii–xix.

14 David Sylvester, Bacon Interviews, 23 April 1975, transcript, Tate Archive, p.15.
15 Joseph de Maistre, *The Works of Joseph de Maistre*, selected and translated by Jack Lively, London 1965, p.291.
16 Ibid., p.294.
17 Ibid., p.192.
18 Sylvester 1997a, p.182
19 In conversation with the author, summer 2000.

BACON'S DIFFERENCE

1 Quoted in Andrew Brighton and Lynda Morris, *Towards Another Picture: An Anthology of Writings by Artists Working in Britain 1945–1977*, Nottingham 1977, p.100.
2 Sir Lawrence Gowing, 'Francis Bacon', in *Francis Bacon: Paintings 1945–1982*, exh. cat., National Museum of Modern Art, Tokyo 1983, p.21.
3 Victor Pasmore, 'The Artists Speaks', *Art News and Review*, vol.3, no.2, 1951.
4 Leif Sjoberg, 'Questions to Victor Pasmore', in *Victor Pasmore*, exh. cat., Durham 1960.
5 Georges Bataille, 'La Bouche', quoted in Dawn Ades, 'Web of Images', in *Francis Bacon*, exh. cat., Tate Gallery, London 1985, p.13.
6 Wyndham Lewis, 'Round the Galleries: Francis Bacon', in *Wyndham Lewis on Art: Collected Writings 1913–1956*, ed. Walter Michel and C. J. Fox, London 1969, pp.393–4.
7 Sylvester 1997a, p.114.
8 Albert Herbert, letter to

the author, June 1999, Tate Gallery Archives.

9 Francis Bacon, 'A Painters Tribute', in *Mathew Smith*, exh. cat., Tate Gallery, London 1953.

10 'Transcript of a conversation between Richard Hamilton, David Alan Mellor and Nicola Roberts', in *The Barry Joule Archive*, 2000, p.30.

11 Sylvester 1997a, p.125

12 David Sylvester, *About Modern Art: Critical Essays 1948–97*, London 1997b, p.16.

13 John Berger, 'Francis Bacon and Walt Disney', in *About Looking*, London 1980, pp.111–18.

14 Alley and Rothenstein 1964.

15 Berlin 1979, p.60.

16 Sylvester 1997a, p.58.

17 R.B. Kitaj, *The Human Clay: An Exhibition Selected by R.B. Kitaj*, exh. cat., Hayward Gallery, London 1976, p.5.

18 Clement Greenberg, 'Modernist Painting', in *Clement Greenberg: The Collected Essays and Criticism, Volume IV: Modernism with a Vengeance, 1957–1969*, ed. John O'Brian, Chicago and London 1993, pp.85–93.

19 Clement Greenberg, '1968: Interview Conducted by Edward Lucie-Smith', in Greenberg 1993, p.278.

20 Clement Greenberg, 'The New Sculpture', in *Art and Culture: Critical Essays*, Boston 1965, p.139.

21 Georg Lukács, *The Meaning of Contemporary Realism*, London 1962, p.20.

CRUCIFIXIONS

1 Sylvester 1997a, p.46.

2 Ades 1985, p.13.

3 Martin Hammer, *Francis Bacon and Nazi Propoganda*, London 2012, pp.13–14.

4 Sylvester 1997b, p.177.

5 Sylvester, Ibid., p.173.

6 Sylvester 1997a, p.13.

7 Peppiatt 1996, p.190.

8 Peter Fuller, 'Raw Bacon', in *Images of God: The Consolation of Lost Illusions*, London 1985, pp.63–70.

9 Michael Leiris, *Francis Bacon: Full Face and in Profile*, Barcelona 1987, p.17.

10 Sylvester 1997a, p.64.

ILLUSTRATION AND THE DYER TRIPTYCHS

1 Sylvester 1997a, p.152.

2 Clement Greenberg, 'Picasso at Seventy-Five', in *Art and Culture: Critical Essays*, Boston 1967, p.62.

3 Gilles Deleuze, *Francis Bacon: The Logic of Sensation*, London 2004.

4 Quoted in Max Kozloff, 'Critical Schizophrenia and the Intentionalist Method', in *Renderings*, London 1968, pp.301–2.

5 Ernst van Alphen, *Francis Bacon and the Loss of Self*, Cambridge, Mass. 1993, p.56.

6 Sylvester 1997a, p.18.

7 Roman Jakobson, quoted in Terry Eagleton, *Literary Theory: An Introduction*, Oxford 1983, p.2.

ERIC HALL AND THE POETS

1 Sylvester 1997a, p.152.

2 T.S. Eliot, 'The Waste Land, 1922', in *Collected Poems 1909–1962*, London 1974, pp.79, 86.

3 Richard Wollheim, *F.H. Bradley*, Harmondsworth 1959.

4 Eric Hall, Jewish Refugees in England, Letter to the Editor, *Times*, Saturday, 30 Sept, 1933, p.11.

5 David Sylvester, 'Review', in *Looking Back at Francis Bacon*, London 2000, pp.19–22.

6 William Bedell Stanford, Aeschylus in his *Style: A Study in Language and Personality*, Dublin 1942, p.13.

7 Ezra Pound, *Literary Essays of Ezra Pound*, ed. T.S. Eliot, London 1960, p.4.

8 T.S. Eliot, 'Tradition and the Individual Talent', in *The Sacred Wood: Essays on Poetry and Criticism*, London 1972, p.54.

9 David Sylvester, Bacon Interviews, 23 April 1975, transcript, Tate Archive, p.13.

BACON'S DELAY

1 Interview with Barry Joule, 'Bacon: A Personal Memoir', *Art Review*, December/ January 1999, pp.30–4.

2 Sylvester 1997a, p.104.

3 Lee Seldes, *The Legacy of Mark Rothko: An Exposé of the Greatest Art Scandal of Our Century*, Harmondsworth 1979, p.263.

4 Francis Bacon, *In Conversation with Michael Archimbaud*, London 1993, p.28.

5 David Sylvester, 'Biographical Note', in *Francis Bacon: The Human Body*, 1998, p.98.

SELECT BIBLIOGRAPHY

Hugh Davies, *Francis Bacon: The early and Middle Years, 1929-1958*, New York 1979.

John Russel, *Francis Bacon*, London 1979.

Ernst van Alphen, *Francis Bacon and the Loss of Self*, Cambridge, Mass. 1993

Michael Peppiatt, *Francis Bacon: Anatomy of an Enigma*, London 1996.

David Sylvester, *Interviews with Francis Bacon 1962–1979*, London 1997.

Mathew Gale, *Francis Bacon: Working on Paper*, exh. cat., Tate Gallery, London 1999.

David Sylvester, *Looking Back at Francis Bacon*, London 2000.

Margarita Cappock, *Francis Bacon's Studio*, London 2005.

Martin Harrison, *In Camera – Francis Bacon: Photography, Film and the Practice of Painting*, London 2005.

Mathew Gale and Chris Stephens, *Francis Bacon*, exh. cat.,Tate Britain, London 2008.

Martin Hammer, *Francis Bacon and Nazi Propoganda*, London, 2012.

ACKNOWLEDGEMENTS

Some people listed below have helped by brief conversations, some by more protracted debates, some by papers they have given, and others have helped directly with my research and comments on the text: Dawn Ades, Ernst van Alphen, Bruce Bernard, Janice Blackburn, Catherine Brighton, Jocelyn Campbell, John E. Costello, Marc Cousins, William Feaver, Wilson Firth, Sarah Fox Pitt, Mathew Gale, Martin Hammer, Christopher Heathcote, Albert Herbert, Richard Humphreys, Sylvia Lahav, John Lavery, David Mellor, Alex Sainsbury, Rory Snookes, Julian Stallabrass, Juliet Steyn, David Sylvester and Jon Thompson. I learnt much from the attendees of the Bacon Course at the Tate Gallery in 1999 and the contributors to sessions on Bacon convened by Dr Martin Hammer at the Association of Art Historians Annual Conference 2000. The librarians at the Tate and Clare Hopkins, Archivist, Trinity College, Oxford, have been a great help. I hope my debt to the writings of others, particularly Michael Peppiatt's biography, is clear in the text and apparatus of this book.

PHOTOGRAPHIC CREDITS

COPYRIGHT CREDITS

INDEX

Abstract Expressionism 69
abstract painting 39, 57, 59
Abstraction 26; fig.12
Ades, Dawn 42, 64
Aeschylus, *Oresteia* 11, 85–6
After Muybridge... 15, 73; fig.3
Alley, Ronald 13, 55
Alphen, Ernst van 77
Andrews, Michael 57
Aristotle, *De Anima* 17
Ashbourne, 2nd Baron 28–9
atomic bomb 9
Auden, W.H. 17, 42
Auerbach, Frank 57
autobiographical elements 71–3, 80–2
autobiographical statements 7, 13

Bacon, Captain Edward
    (father) 12–13, 15–16
Bacon, Francis
    asthma 15
    atheism 6, 9, 12, 29, 32, 54
    childhood 11–16, 18
    death 6, 91
    education 15, 17
    family 8, 11–12, 15–17
    homosexuality 7, 13, 16, 17
    intellect 23, 56
    masochistic sexuality 16, 71
    persona 6, 13, 17, 18, 22
    studio 7
Bacon, Winifred (mother) 12, 15, 16
Bataille, Georges 42, 64
Baudelaire, Charles 29; fig.16
Beckett, Samuel 61
Beckmann, Max 18
Berger, John 50, 52, 54, 56
Berlin 17, 18
Berlin, Isaiah 28, 56
Bernard, Bruce 32
Bloomsbury Group 17
Bradley, F.H. 83–4
Brausen, Erica 37, 90
Buhler, Robert 54

Capéllo, José 91
Chirico, Giorgio de 21
Cimabue 71
Colony Club 50
Composition (Figure) 24; fig.8
Connolly, Cyril 10
Croce, Benedetto 22
Crucifixion (1933) 30; figs.14, 15
Crucifixion (1965) 72–4; fig.43
crucifixion motif 30, 63–74

Dadaists 18
de Maistre, Roy 23–7, 30, 55
    Figure by a Bath 26; fig.11
    Studio Interior 24, 26; fig.9
Deakin, John, *Portrait of
    George Dyer* 82; fig.50

Degas, Edgar 37, 44, 87
    After the Bath… 67; fig.40
Deleuze, Giles 76, 79, 80
despair, ideologies of
    11, 18, 21–34
Dix, Otto 18
Documents magazine 42
Duchamp, Marcel 18, 90
Dyer, George 67, 80–2; fig.50
Dyer triptychs 77–82

Edwards, John 91
Eisenstein, Sergei, *Battleship
    Potemkin* 42
Eliot, T.S. 21, 26, 29, 61,
    83, 84, 85, 86–7
Epstein, Jacob 85
Eumenides 11, 64, 67, 73
Existentialism 9

figurative painting 39, 42,
    52, 60–1, 75–82, 86
*Figure Getting out of a
    Car* 26, 55–6; fig.29
Figure in a Landscape 56; fig.31
Fragments of a Crucifixion
    64, 67, 74; 38
Freud, Lucian 57, 59, 85
    Francis Bacon 59; fig.32
    portrait by Bacon 44; fig.21
Freud, Sigmund 16, 18, 56
Fuller, Peter 72
Furies *see* Eumenides

Gaudier-Brzeska, Henri 86
Genet, Jean, *The Balcony* 74
Georges Carpentier 47; fig.23
glass, Bacon's use of 61, 87
Gowing, Lawrence 35, 39
Greenberg, Clement 59–61,
    75–6, 79, 82, 87
Grosz, George 18
Grünewald, Mathis
    Christ Carrying the Cross fig.16
    Mocking of Christ 11

Hall, Eric 23, 56, 84–5
Hamilton, Richard 46
Hammer, Martin 67, 71, 85
Harpies 67
Head I 39, 42; fig.19
*Head IV (Man with
    Monkey)* 37–8; fig.17
Head VI 42; fig.20
Herbert, Albert 44–5
Hesiod 67
Höch, Hannah 18
Horizon magazine 9–11, 85
Hunter, Sam, photographs of
    Bacon's studio 54; fig.16

illustration/narrative
    readings 75–7, 81–2
Impressionism 39, 61
interior design 21, 22; fig.7
Ireland 11–16
Isherwood, Christopher 29

Jakobson, Roman 82
Jewish terrorism in Palestine 64
Joule, Barry 23, 89, 91
    Portrait of Francis Bacon
    89; frontispiece, fig.53
Joyce, James 61

Kafka, Franz 44, 61
Kant, Immanuel 59–60
Keynes, Maynard 22–3
Kitaj, R.B. 57, 59
    Synchrony with F B 59; fig.33
Kossoff, Leon 57

Lacey, Peter 71
Lamennais, Abbé de 29
Laocoön and his Two Sons 82
Le Corbusier 21
Léger, Fernand 21
Leiris, Michel 73
Lewis, Wyndham 42, 44
London 17, 21
Lord, James 10

Lukács, Georg 61, 83

MacMurray, Betty 24
Maistre, Joseph de 27–32, 56
Man in a Cap 54; fig.28
Marlborough Fine Art 13, 90–1
Marr, David 24
Masaryk, Jan 67
Maurras, Charles 29
Maxwell, Marius, *Stalking Big
    Game with a Camera...* fig.16
Maybury, John, *Love is the Devil* 81
Melville, Robert 10
Michelangelo 37, 44, 87
Minton, John 44
Miss Muriel Belcher 50; fig.27
modernism 8, 10, 17, 21,
    22–3, 57, 59–61
Mondrian, Piet 61
Mortimer, Raymond 11
Moyne, Lord 64
Moynihan, Rodrigo 44
    Portrait Group 45, 54; fig.22
Munnings, Alfred 13, 22, 44
    *My Wife, My Horse &
    Myself* 13; fig.2
Muybridge, Eadweard 15, 37, 44
    Athletes Wrestling fig.36
    Infantile Paralysis... 15; fig.4

Nash, Paul 21
Nazis and Nazi imagery 18, 54–5,
    63–4, 67, 71, 73–4; fig.16
Neo-Romanticism 9
New Statesman journal 50, 52
New York School 87
Nietzsche, Friedrich 9

Painting (1946) 30, 63–4, 74; fig.37
painting technique 37–9, 44–7, 50, 61
Paris 17
Pasmore, Victor 39
    Spiral Motif 39; fig.18
Pater, Walter 17
Peppiatt, Michael 16, 17, 18, 71
photography 48–9

Bacon's use of 35, 37,
    42, 44, 46–7, 54–6, 79,
    89–90; figs.16, 23
Picasso, Pablo 17, 18, 21, 22, 24,
    37, 75, 87, 90
    Baigneuse 30; fig.14
    biomorphic works 11, 18, 24;
    fig.14
    The Three Dancers 30,
    75–6, 82; figs.13, 51
Picture Post magazine fig.16
Pink Crawling Figure 47; fig.24
Poe, Edgar Allan 29
pope series 42, 55, 63
Portrait of Isabel Rawsthorne
    60–1; fig.34
Portrait of John Edwards 91; fig.52
Portrait of Lucian Freud 44; fig.21
Portrait of R.J. Sainsbury 50; fig.26
portraits 48–50
Pound, Ezra 86
Poussin, Nicolas, *The Massacre
    of the Innocents* 42
Proust, Marcel 61
Purism 21

Read, Herbert 18
    Art Now 22, 30; fig.14
realism 30, 32
Reclining Woman 69; fig.42
Rembrandt van Rijn 37, 87
    Self-Portrait 76; fig.44
Rodin, Auguste 37
    The Thinker fig.16
Rothenstein, Sir John 13, 26–7
Royal College of Art
    44–5, 54; fig.22
Russell, John 13, 22, 23
Ryan, Adrian 7

Sade, Marquis de 10
School of London 57, 59
screaming/shouting mouth
    motif 39, 42, 54–6, 63
Seldes, Lee 91
sexuality in Bacon's work 17–18

Sitwell, Osbert 9
Smith, Matthew 46
Sontag, Susan 50
Stanford, William Bedell 85–6
The Studio magazine 21; fig.7
Surrealism 75, 86
Sutherland, Graham 9, 11
    Somerset Maugham 76; fig.45
Sylvester, David 7, 8, 11,
    12, 16–17, 23, 50, 52,
    63, 68, 69, 70, 86
Synthetic Cubism 61

Three Figures and Portrait 67; fig.39
Three Studies for a Crucifixion
    67–72, 74; fig.41
*Three Studies for Figures at
    the Base of a Crucifixion*
    (c.1944) 11, 23, 26, 56, 67,
    71, 85–6; figs.1, 5, 30
*Three Studies for Figures at the
    Base of a Crucifixion* (1988) 72
*Three Studies of the Human
    Head* 47; fig.25
transgressions 8
*Triptych Inspired by T.S. Eliot's Poem
    'Sweeney Agonistes'* 24, 26; fig.10
Triptych May–June 1973 81; fig.48
*Triptych – In Memory of George
    Dyer* 77–83; figs.46, 49
triptychs 68, 70
Two Figures 61; fig.35

Valéry, Paul 76
van Gogh, Vincent 87
    *Painter on the Road
    to Tarascon* 68–9
Velázquez, Diego 37, 42
    Pope Innocent X 42; fig.16

Watercolour (1929) 21–2; fig.6
White, Patrick 17, 24, 27

X Album fig.47